D0483982

Deeper Walk

A Relevant Devotional Series

VOLUME 1

GOD OF THE DESERT, GOD OF GREATNESS

edited by
Winn Collier

Published by Relevant Books
A division of Relevant Media Group, Inc.

www.relevantbooks.com
www.relevantmediagroup.com

© 2003 by Relevant Media Group, Inc.

Design by Relevant Solutions
Bobby Jones, Raul Justiniano, Daniel Ariza, Greg Lutze
www.relevant-solutions.com

Relevant Books is a registered trademark of Relevant Media Group, Inc.,
and is registered in the U.S. Patent and Trademark Office.

Library of Congress Control Number: 2002109732
International Standard Book Number: 0-9714576-5-4

For information:
RELEVANT MEDIA GROUP, INC.
POST OFFICE BOX 951127
LAKE MARY, FL 32795
407-333-7152

03 04 05 06 9 8 7 6 5 4 3 2 1

Printed in the United States of America

Deeper Walk

A Relevant Devotional Series

VOLUME 1

GOD OF THE DESERT,
GOD OF GREATNESS

edited by
Winn Collier

CONTENTS

CONTENTS

PREFACE

I must confess: I'm generally not drawn to modern devotional books. They often strike me as trite or trendy, ramblings rarely connected to the aches of my soul. I yearn to glimpse behind the veil of mystery.

My eyes of faith pull me to step over the threshold, into the realm of my transcendent God. On this side of the veil, it seems paradox, childlike wonder, and questions are often unwelcome. So, we must move. We must step into God. In faith, we must cross over. Unfortunately, our guides on this side offer us little help. Spiritual formulas, ever-ready answers, and the familiar barrage of words are unable to chart our course. They don't know the terrain on the other side. They are unfamiliar with its vocabulary. They know little of mystery. Only vaguely aware of the realm behind the veil, it has never even occurred to them to take a peek.

I am not alone. There is a growing company of God-seekers, discontent with words *about* God, hungry for an experience *with* God. They do not presume that God can be defined or categorized. Sensing we have trivialized God, they want to go deeper. They want to explore the fathoms of the Deep One. They sense He is both near and far. He is the ultimate paradox, and He ignites our worship.

It is for these cravers of God that we have gathered this collection of devotional writings. I have come to think of them as meditations for the hungry soul. This collection is only a beginning, an introductory guide. God is the pursuit of our life, and He will reveal Himself to the hungry heart. But each revelation will only whet our appetite. It will leave us wanting more.

Author Kathleen Norris knew this bewildering reality. In *Cloister Walk*, she lamented, "With God there is always more unfolding … What we can glimpse of the divine is always exactly enough, and never enough."

Truly, what we will taste of God will never be enough. It will meet our need; it will bring us joy in our moment of connection. It will comfort us to know there is the possibility that our hearts' deepest thirst can be quenched. It will flood us with pleasure. But it will not be enough.

It will draw us deeper in. It will ask us to trust more. To feel more. To dare more. To believe more. To risk more. To want more.

With God, there is always more.

So we set off, following the path after Him. We must.
Nothing else offers such hope. No one else speaks
such words.

The journey is long. The ancient path that follows after
Him is well trodden. Though many miles can only be
walked in solitude, you will also meet many friends along
the way. Listen to them. Join with them. Open your
heart, and share the Savior together. And when the time
comes to walk another stretch alone, say "farewell."

The road will offer many unexpected bends, traversing a
landscape that you, at times, may find daunting and
unfamiliar. Carry on. Your God is with you. Your God
will guide you.

You will encounter moments when you will wonder if it
is worth it. Have you made a foolish decision; have you
chosen too difficult a path? It is hard, and you will question God's silence. At times, you will look back. You may
even step back. Carry on. The path leads to the heart of
God, and every step, every mile, is a little bit closer.

So, carry on. Step forward. Go deeper. Wade past the
shallow waters that have allowed you to drift aimlessly,
close to the shore but far from the depths of God.

In this volume, we simply hope that you find a friend or
two to help you peer behind the veil and to step over to

the other side. We hope you find a little rest in your journey. We hope it helps you move closer and swim deeper.

And may God's words to Kathleen Norris be the voice you hear as you plunge in: "You are entering the deep, uncharted waters."

Winn Collier, editor

GOD
OF
THE
DESERT

⊰IN BETWEEN⊱
Margaret Feinberg

There's a place between here and there. A piece of ground in the middle of take-off and landing. A section of the unknown within beginning and ending. You probably find yourself there from time to time. It's the land known as *Inbetween*.

Inbetween is one of the most rugged places in life. You aren't fully here, and you aren't fully there. Your emotions and hopes are strewn across an endless list of possibilities. Door knobs of wood, brass, and silver line the path, but which will open? In the land of *Inbetween*, the paths are lined with sealed envelopes and foggy dreams. Excitement runs forward and fears hold back. And if you stay long enough, you feel the tremors of your soul.

The land of *Inbetween* is downright scary. It's a place of blind trust. It's where the pedals of faith meet the narrow road of fortitude and where movement is demanded though there's no place to go. The worst part about this land isn't the uncertainty or frustration that accompany it—it's that God likes it when you're there.

While He's no sadist, God loves the land of *Inbetween*. He loves what it does to us. He loves the humility and dependence it creates in our hearts, so He creates innumerable forks in life's road that swerve us into the land of *Inbetween*. The unknowns of job, marriage, children, and home are the road signs of this uncertain land. At times, people are thrust into *Inbetween* by mishaps, accidents, sudden deaths, and even unexpected fortune. Some people visit so many times they begin to wonder if it's life. And they aren't far off.

So what will hold you steady when you walk through the terrain of *Inbetween*? A recognition that *Inbetween* is God's design. In one miraculous moment, the Creator of the universe placed you in the greatest *Inbetween* of all time—the place between this earthy creation and eternity. Life's smaller lunges forward and backward are merely postcard reminders that there's something greater than this place we're visiting.

If you're in your own land of *Inbetween*, remember that God was the original designer of this journey. You can get mad, scream and even pout if you want. But it doesn't change the fact that you're merely passing through. Everything else is *Inbetween*.

EVEN DEEPER
Read about the stages of Israel's journey in Numbers 33, then draw a time line of your life. Mark significant dates on it. Reflect on how far God has brought you. Ponder Psalm 23:4.

PRAYER
Father, my heart longs for eternity but my body remains here. Help me to see life as a journey that is completed through communion with You.

⊰MEETING GOD IN THE DUNGEON⊱
Doug Floyd

Joseph awoke to the nightmare that his life had become.
Buried in the damp, deep, and dark earth, he found himself enrolled in a school he never heard about or ever
registered to attend. He found himself in the Spiritual
School of the Suffering.

In the dark loneliness of suffering, Joseph dreamed of
redemption. Joseph had always been a dreamer.

His dreams were subversive. His dreams were what started this whole mess. He dreamed that the powerful would
bow down to the weak. As the favored son of Jacob,
Joseph had one too many dreams that he would be
greater than even his own brothers. Betrayed by his own
blood, Joseph was sold as a slave.

He dreamed he would become a great slave. Once again,
his dreamed proved fateful. Betrayed by his master's wife,
Joseph found his integrity rewarded with imprisonment.

Prisons can be great places for dreaming. In the dark
loneliness of suffering, Joseph dreamed. Joseph was
beaten, betrayed, and forgotten, but not dead.
Day after day, week after week, year after year, Joseph
waited. And hoped. And dreamed.

Joseph was not forsaken.

The spirituality of the dungeon is not popular. Not too many books are written on meeting God in the dungeon. In a culture of pampering and pleasure, suffering is not en vogue.

Despite its unpopularity, many who follow after God have spent many days in the dungeon. The Scriptures are filled with real stories of real people enduring great suffering. The Bible is nearly silent as to why. Job loses everything or why Joseph is stranded in the pits of a dungeon.

Some will suffer, curse God, and die. Inwardly, they cut themselves off from all hope. Yet some will suffer greatly and see a light of hope beyond the darkness. They will learn to delight in the gentle glimpses of God's grace. In the heart of suffering, in the center of the cross, there is an intimacy with God only sufferers will enjoy.

EVEN DEEPER
Reflect upon Romans 5:2-4, 8:18, and Acts 16:24-26. Evaluate how you are handling your points of suffering. Are you allowing it to take you to the heart of God? This week, explore how God may be moving through your dungeon experiences.

PRAYER
God, be my God … even in the dungeon.

THE DESERT ROMANCE

Doug Floyd

Desert spirituality seems almost romantic: the journey into the unknown. It is fascinating to read stories of Abraham and Elijah and their times of soul-searching in the wilderness. But danger awaits in the desert, oppressive and life threatening. Death is not romantic. It reminds us we are weak and needy.

The desert is exile.

Moses knew the desert. He lived most of his life wandering in forsaken wasteland. Moses abandoned his adopted royal family when he chose to defend a persecuted brother. The desert was his reward. Exiled, Moses roamed the wilderness as a nomadic shepherd.

One day, standing in the middle of the desert heat, the nameless nomad turned to meet the Unfathomable One. Facing the blazing bush, he heard, "Moses!" The piercing voice reminded him of his name: He was the "drawn out" one. As a baby, he was drawn out of the waters, rescued. That day, standing there, he was being drawn out of the desert, a tool of God to rescue His people.

Standing on holy ground, he faced the God of his ancestors, the God who Moses thought had abandoned him in the desert a lifetime ago. Moses asked, "What is your name?" but got no name. To this day, we still do not understand what was said to him. Some suggest the voice said, "I am I am," or possibly, "I am and remain present." This God cannot be summoned—He has never been gone. He is Present.

Moses was never alone. All those years he had wandered, believing he had been forsaken. But he was never forsaken. God is Present. In His presence, the desert becomes a sanctuary, a holy temple. Moses learned what we must learn. We are not forsaken or alone. God is present.His never-failing Word accompanies us in the desert, even as we face its pains, heat, and loneliness.

Every day we face the possibility of dying in the desert. The struggles of life threaten to crush the essence of who we were created to be. In the desert, we face our weakness, but there we find His strength. We must learn to look to God as He calls out our name. Like Moses, we listen to His call and remember.

EVEN DEEPER
Read Deuteronomy 2:7 and 31:1-8. Are you in the desert? Spend a few quiet moments with God. Face Him. Ask Him to tell you your name.

PRAYER
God of the desert, You are present. When it seems I am alone and the despair of the desert begins to swallow me, remind me, God—remind me that You have never left. Even now, You call my name.

❧THE SEDUCTION OF HAPPINESS❧

Garry Geer

I am sure you have felt it. Prayer is a chore. The Bible is tedious. Worship becomes a necessary actcivity we are obligated to participate in.

I think spiritual boredom arises from a quest for happiness versus a quest for joy. Fulfilling a momentary impulse brings about happiness. It's easy. It's quick. We don't have to think about it. Depressed? Go see a movie. Frustrated? Go participate in a recreational pasttime until endorphins and good spirits drown that irritating nag.

This is not to say that happiness is wrong, but it falls prey to the basic rules of human sensation. The law of diminishing returns doesn't just apply to drug users. Anytime we seek to relive the pleasure that arose from a spontaneous moment, we will not be able to gain the same satisfaction. Happiness also acts as the ultimate placebo. Having a problem with a friend? A situation arising at your job that you really don't want to think about? As the old song goes, "Come on, get happy." But like any placebo, while the symptom may have gone away, the root of the problem still remains.

As Christians, we have bought into one of society's big lies. We have made happiness the end goal, living as though we are the center of the universe. With this belief, we ignore the true purpose of our existence: to glorify God.

"coffee prune your
to best for you" —best,
is best
for you

Sometimes glorifying God doesn't make us "happy." It requires us to look outside of ourselves and search for that most desired, yet least understood state: joy.

Joy demands a bit of effort. It asks that I be satisfied with God's sovereign working in my life. It doesn't offer the same short-term emotional pay-off that happiness does, but ultimately it changes me at a foundational level. Joy results from the obedience that arises from my understanding and appreciation of God's holiness and love. It happens when I enter into prayer cold, yet later arise changed by time spent with Him confessing, arguing, and ultimately submitting.

The times when we are bored with God are the times when we are concerned about momentary stimuli, moving from entertainment to entertainment like a honeybee from flower to flower. God doesn't desire that we live for the moment, but rather that we live for eternity.

EVEN DEEPER
Take a good look at what you spend your days longing for: the passing excitement of happiness or the sustaining pleasure of joy. Meditate on Psalm 39:7, John 12:25, and Romans 12:2.

PRAYER
God, how could I be so wrapped up in the moment that I miss the eternal? I don't want to live with such a shortsighted view. Help me to be wrapped up in the joy only You bring.

⊰WITHOUT THESE TRIALS⊱

Margaret Feinberg

Without these trials, I would claim to know the depth and warmth of Your embrace but would be unable to extend it to others.

Without these trials, I wouldn't know the extent of Your goodness or appreciate the countless sunny days and smooth seas You've given me in the past.

Without these trials, I wouldn't be able to comfort others, empathize with them, or understand the depths of their despair.

Without these trials, I would still think I had all the answers and would be closed off to Your correction and molding.

Without these trials, I wouldn't be dependent, humble, or quiet, nor would Your character be developing in me.

Without these trials, the darkness would never come, and I would never be given the opportunity to shine like the sun.

Without these trials, I would begin to wonder if I was truly Your beloved and would settle for lesser lovers.

Without these trials, I wouldn't grow stronger, have a stiffer backbone, or be able to face hardship at all.

Without these trials, I wouldn't have anything to present to You except a few sticks, some stubble, and a handful of hay.

Without these trials, hope would seem shallow, faith would seem weak, and love would seem impossible.

Without these trials, my faith, which is more precious than gold, would never grow into all You've created it to be.

So in the midst, I thank You for these trials.

EVEN DEEPER
What have been the major trials of your life?
What fruit have they offered? Ponder James 1:12.

PRAYER
Father, I ask for the grace to endure the trials You've allowed in my life. I ask for the strength to overcome them and bring glory to Your name. I love You.

NOWHERE ELSE TO GO
Steph Gehring

Nothing would make Satan happier than putting God's army out of commission by convincing us to let him take our will to live, laugh, be glad, work, and love. Despair isn't something we simply "snap out of." However, it is a battle we can fight, emotionally and spiritually. Attacking our minds, Satan turns our souls into a battleground. The temptation is to completely turn to ourselves, thinking we must either win the fight alone or fall, exhausted, in silence.

Often when we turn to God for answers about these matters of the soul, we end up with more questions than we started with. Even Jesus' disciples, the ones who walked and ate with God, who felt Love's breath on their cheeks—even they were often confused. And yet, even in this confusion, He is the only trustworthy One, the only One to whom we can turn. It's a child-like faith.

While He may not provide all the answers, He does not leave us to struggle alone. He struggles with us.

In John 6, Jesus asked a penetrating question in the face of His friends' doubt: "You don't want to leave me, too, do you?" In other words, "Are you finished with me, ready to go look for a Messiah who punishes those who cause you pain, who proves you right instead of asking you hard questions, who gives you the answers you seek and makes your problems go away? Have you lost the will to follow my confusing footsteps, to give up your dreams and let God dream through you instead?"

Peter's answer was as raw as the question: "Lord, to whom shall we go?" Another way of saying, "We'd go look if we thought there were anyone else, but there isn't. Only you have the words of eternal life. You are all we have."

And He is.

We should want to be like Peter, clinging to truth even in doubt. Let's follow Him, even to a cross. Let's let go of our hearts and lay them in His hands without demanding guarantees.

If we choose God, we choose life. And anything other than God is death.

EVEN DEEPER
Read Psalm 118:8, Matthew 10:39, and John 10:10. Are you sensing despair? Remove your masks. Be honest with your heart. Where are you sensing pain? Sit down with your wounds, pull out a journal, and talk to God about them. He will be listening.

PRAYER
Lord, where else can we go? You are all we have. You are all we need.

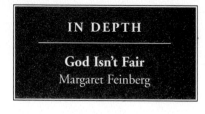
God isn't fair. Millions of children die. Family members suffer with cancer. Murderers go free. Wouldn't a God who was fair respond? These situations cause the child within us to well up and scream, "Unfair!" Together, these untamed voices proclaim to the world that God isn't fair and therefore isn't a good God.

Even biblical characters faced this issue. If anyone knew God's unfairness, it was Zechariah. Not the man who climbed the Sycamore tree, but the one married to Elizabeth, Mary's sister. He was a devout man. He made it his vocation to serve God. He was a priest in the division of Abijah, and, like very few described in the Bible, was "righteous in the sight of God, walking blameless in all the commandments and requirements of the Lord." (When was the last time someone described you with these qualities?) he was a man who pleased God in all that he did.

The only thing the Bible tells us Zechariah ever wanted was to have a child. In the early years of their marriage, he and Elizabeth were hopeful and optimistic. But as the years passed, the reality set in that they might never have one.

Yet Zechariah persevered; he did everything a man knows to do to help his wife become pregnant. And he prayed—the Bible says he "petitioned" God. But all he heard was silence. Month after month. Year after year. He continued to meet all the commandments and requirements of the Lord. He prayed. He sought heaven. But no child. His wife felt the disgrace; her neighbors whispered about their lack of favor.

Were they doing something wrong? Had they missed God? The answer from heaven was silence. As their bodies began to sag, and as gray hair and wrinkles replaced a once youthful appearance, Zechariah and Elizabeth accepted the fact that there was no one to carry on their lineage. Their mothers stopped asking if Elizabeth was pregnant. Their neighbors turned to other nuggets of gossip. And the only children their home enjoyed were those of visiting relatives.

Zechariah had every reason to raise his finger to God's unfairness. Why did those who didn't serve in the priesthood have children? Why did those who practiced harlotry nurse babes? Why did those who stole from the temple enjoy grandchildren? Why? But Zechariah remained as silent as heaven on these issues.

That is, until one ordinary day when he was chosen to serve in the temple. As the whole multitude waited in prayer outside, he entered to perform his priestly duty. But there was something different about the inner room as he stepped in. He gasped. An angel was standing to the right of the altar. Fear gripped Zechariah's being. He wanted to coil in a ball on the floor but was paralyzed with a silent tremor. A thundering but calm voice told him not be afraid. Heaven had heard his plea. Elizabeth would have a son who would be great in the sight of the Lord and prepare the way for His arrival. The words seemed too good to be true. Looking down at his weak-ened, frail body, he stammered, "How shall I know for certain? For I am an old man, and my wife is advanced in years?"

It was a fair question for an unfairly common situation. But the answer was more than a rebuke. It was a judg-ment. Gabriel sternly replied, "You shall be silent and unable to speak until the day when these things take place, because you did not believe my words, which shall be fulfilled in their proper time."

"But ..." Zechariah began to stammer. Nothing came out of his mouth. Instantly, he was mute. As he stepped out of the temple, the crowd bombarded him with questions. "What took you so long?" and "What happened in there?" But all he could do was shake his hands and head in an unsuccessful game of charades. After completing the following days of his priestly service, the devout man returned home with his wife. As promised, she became pregnant. "Congratulations," you may say with a smile. But remember, Zechariah is mute. He can't speak. There are no stories. No conversations. No real explanations. Only silence, the same silence he heard from heaven all those years.

And for what? For simply asking the angel to give him a sign. Mary had the sign of Elizabeth's birth. The wise men had the star. The multitudes had bread and fish multiplied. But Zechariah was struck mute. Was it fair? Absolutely not. Our sense of fairness will always be challenged by the eyes of a just God.

For the next nine months, Zechariah couldn't talk. But he could watch. He could listen. He could notice things he had never seen before. In his silence, he had more time than ever to listen to God, learn from others, and notice things for the first time. Most importantly, he had time to watch God fulfill His promises and increase his faith and time to grow in his relationship with Him.

How do we know that the time of silence—the judgment that seemed impossible to bear—wasn't actually a blessing? Because after his mouth was loosed, Zechariah said four little words, "His name is John," and then began praising God. Sound like a man who is disenchanted? Frustrated with God's faithfulness? Angry with His reasoning?

No, it sounds like a man who embraced God's judgment for all it was worth and benefited from it. It sounds like a man who took what most of us would consider evil and recognized it as good. It sounds like a man who walked righteously in the sight of God. He knew God wasn't fair. But he also knew that God was just. And in his childlike faith, he became the father of John the Baptist—the forerunner of Jesus Christ.

⊰A NEW NAME⊱
Allison Foley

A year away from finishing college, we begin to think about our "callings" in life. It is confusing. Each time we think we know where we are supposed to be going, our lives change course. Life is often a wrestling match between what we think (or hope) God wants, and the reality of His direction for us.

Jacob must have faced something similar when he wrestled with God at Peniel. God won the match and dislocated his hip. Jacob fought hard, but he didn't win. He didn't get what he wanted from God. This "dislocation" in our own lives causes pain and frustration. Where are we going? What are we doing? We question ourselves. We question our connection with God. Does God hate me? Did I do something wrong?

Jacob emerged from the wrestling match with more than a dislocated hip. He got a new name—Israel—a name God picked out for Jacob. It embodied Jacob's true identity, an unexpected blessing from wrestling with God.

God often allows difficulties into our lives right before moving or ushering us into a new level in our relationship with Him. Deep down we want to believe God is still there. But it doesn't seem like He is when He's dislocating your hip or shaking the things you thought were secure. He wants more of you, and He is willing to wound you to get it.

Maybe God has a different path, and He needs to get your attention to show it to you. Maybe God has something better in store. Maybe God is calling you to walk in a way you haven't tried before, with a hip out of place. Maybe God has a new name He wants to give you, but He has to bring you to a place where you will listen.

EVEN DEEPER
Read Jacob's story: Genesis 32:22-31. Where do you feel like God has "knocked out your hip?" Do you think He may be attempting to get your attention, directing you to something new? Spend some time writing or drawing your thoughts.

PRAYER
Dear God, thank You for being in control of my destination. Give me faith to believe that You are doing more than I see right now. Help me to receive the new name You give me.

⊰WHAT ARE YOU WAITING FOR?⊱
Margaret Feinberg

What are you waiting for? Maybe it's a new, better job, a marriage proposal, a dream vacation? Maybe you're just waiting for the weekend or, more simply, the next thing.

Whatever you're waiting for, the world has an answer. It'll tell you run harder, push faster, make it happen. It'll make you feel like it's okay to be a little compulsive. You only live once, so eat it, flaunt it, charge it. After all, you're worth it. You deserve it. You've only got to take care of yourself.

These are the nuggets of worldly motivation. Society insists we gorge ourselves on them. Because waiting is hard, real hard. Waiting demands we embrace faith. We hold on for opportunity. We carry hope. We trust in something, or rather Someone, greater than ourselves.

Recall the last time you waited. What happened? The answer came. The letter arrived. Another position opened up. Another person came along. And, oh yeah, don't forget, life went on.

So you have a track record. Do you really need to ask if your wait is worth it? Or do you already have a hunch? Most of the greats in the Bible were friends of waiting. John waited his whole life to write the best-selling apocalyptic book of all time, *Revelation*. The Israelites waited forty years to shake the sand from their sandals and enter the Promised Land. Jesus waited thirty years to start His ministry. Jonah sat three days in the stinky belly of a fish before God used him to bring revival to Nineveh.

Do you want renewal? Do you want to minister to others? Do you want an extraordinary son? Do you want an extraordinary job? Do you want an extraordinary spouse? Do you want the extraordinary? Do you want God's best for your life? If so, then you'll probably have to wait. So the next time someone asks you, "What are you waiting for?" smile, and with a twinkle of hope reply, "God."

EVEN DEEPER
Meditate upon Isaiah 64:3-5 and Lamentations 3:23-25. Then use a concordance to study the word patience. What does the Bible tell us its fruits are?

PRAYER
Father, forgive me for my impatience. I trust You, and I want Your best. Help me to wait on You. I love You.

THE GIFT OF BROKENNESS
Melanie Seibert

"The sacrifices of God are a broken spirit; a broken and contrite heart, O God, you will not despise" (Psalm 51:17).

The Great Commission is, at its core, a command to put people in touch with reality. We are told to take the Gospel to all humankind, to tell them the true story of their own smallness and the bigness of the grace of God.

But not everyone is ready to listen. Some look at their lives and see no need to change. They are self-sufficient; they are fulfilled. They have jobs, families, churches, and happy, happy lives. They need nothing.

Although Christians often rightly recognize the needs of the obviously down-and-out—the homeless man, the drug addict, the prostitute, the abused child—sometimes we forget those who seem less desperate, such as the lawyer, the teacher, or the mother who lives in our community. But we are called to show God to each of them, and sharing the Gospel with those who see no need for God may mean introducing them to a disturbing truth: their own brokenness.

But first we must know brokenness ourselves. Our brokenness is a difficult notion to accept for those of us characterized by its opposite: complacency and the assumption that we're okay. We often fail to pursue the thoughtful examination of conscience Paul encourages, and instead, we maintain a thoughtless defensiveness, refusing to consider where we truly stand with God. Complacency is easier than self-examination, easier than humility, and most certainly easier than repentance.

But brokenness is essential. Only in brokenness do we grasp the truth: we're dependent on God because we can't rely upon ourselves. When we're broken, we gain perspective. We lose sight of all the illusions of our own merit and self-sufficiency, which can, at times, distract us from the truth of our own frailty and the value of God's promise of salvation to our broken souls.

EVEN DEEPER
Meditate on Psalm 34:18 and 147:3. Identify the areas of your life where you have not been broken. Thank God for His faithfulness to you even when you didn't recognize it. Think of someone you care for who doesn't recognize his need for God. Pray for God's intervention.

PRAYER
God, keep me in touch with reality. Thank You for my brokenness that reminds me of how much I need You. As for those people in my life who don't realize they need You, please bless them with the gift of brokenness.

BORED WITH GOD

Winn Collier

The adjective I could often use for my spiritual life is *numb*. Such a description doesn't conjure up images of spiritual heroics, but there is a certain noble ring to it.

A weary warrior halts and crouches; in a daze, he scans the charred battlefield. Numb. A grief-stricken woman battles deep loss in the caverns of her soul. Numb. We are often numb because we have fought well. We are weary. Tired. Numb. And that actually sounds pretty valiant.

Unfortunately, however, at times what I really feel is nothing so gallant as numbness. I face a much darker reality. I am bored with God.

You have been there—you want to pursue the Almighty, but all you can manage is a yawn. You take a walk to pray, and the slightest distraction pulls you from the Throne. You plan to use the quiet of your commute to commune with God; and within seconds, everything within you wants to flip on the radio. You don't care if all you can pick up is static—you just need the noise. You can't stand the quiet. It's boring. Bored with God.

Lord Byron seemed to think boredom an inevitable element of proper society: "Society is now one polish'd horde, formed of two mighty tribes, the *Bores* and *Bored*." So, is that how it is? Boredom is inevitable? Just accept it? Bury it, and play the game, pretending your spiritual life runs deep so others won't notice the coldness swallowing your heart?

Boredom may prove inevitable, but it isn't God's design. Jesus said He can live with His followers being hot or cold, but the mucky middle of lukewarm is where the stench brews. Boredom is a polite term for the stench of being unmoved by the grandeur of God.

Boredom reveals something deeper: our hearts have been captured by something other than God. The proper response is not to do more, work harder, or make more commitments. These aren't responses of the heart. The result of endless activity for God is boredom—He has become small, replaced by a focus on our efforts.

We need to reconnect with the romancing God whose story ignites our imagination. We must allow time and space to simply be creatures of our God, listening to His story afresh, sitting at His feet anew, and quieting our hearts in His presence. In time, a fresh awakening will yield. And as we struggle to find words to describe this awakening, *boredom* won't even be considered.

> **EVEN DEEPER**
> Study Romans 12:11-13. What adjectives describe your spiritual life? Write down four or five.
>
> **PRAYER**
> God of Wonder, allow me to be quiet and see You afresh. Capture my heart.

◆STRAWBERRY FIELDS◆

Margaret Feinberg

In his book, *The Ragamuffin Gospel*, Brennan Manning relates a Zen story about a monk who is being pursued by a raging tiger. Forced to the edge of a cliff, the monk discovers a rope hanging over the edge and narrowly escapes the ferocious animal's jaws. Hundreds of feet below, he sees the bottom of the rugged canyon. When he looks up, the tiger is still staring at him, but now two small mice are nibbling on the rope. What should the monk do?

The monk notices a strawberry within arm's length growing on the side of the cliff. Straining, he picks it, eats it, and exclaims, "Yum-yum—that's the best strawberry I've ever tasted!"

Manning points out that if the monk had been preoccupied with the rock below (the future) or the tiger stationed above (the past), he would have missed the strawberry God was giving him at the moment.

God's strawberries are all around us, but we often fail to notice them, pick them, or enjoy their succulent flavor. When we find ourselves between a tiger and a hard place, we often turn to our most primitive instinct: survival. Instead of noticing God's provision for us, we focus on the problem and our need to escape. God has not forgotten us, and He'll even grow strawberries in life's rockiest patches to prove it.

Can you think of any strawberries God has grown for you? They come in different forms, but they have one thing in common: they're easy to overlook. A call from your mom. A spectacular sunset or moon rising. A random letter from an old friend. The announcement of a baby's birth. A sale at your favorite department store. A knee-melting kiss. Ice cream with sprinkles. A smile from a stranger. Scripture that breaths life and delivers hope. A newspaper that arrives two feet closer to your doorstep. Someone who says nothing, but simply listens. Photo albums loaded with some of life's best memories. A walk through the woods. God's strawberries.

Maybe you're in need of a strawberry. If so, keep your eyes open. Don't let raging tigers or jagged rocks distract you. God may have one for you just around the corner. Or maybe you can offer a strawberry to someone else. Pick up the phone. Dust off your stationery collection. Jot a note. Blow up balloons. Offer a quiet prayer. Clip a comic. Someone else could be staring up at a tiger right now.

EVEN DEEPER
Consider Matthew 7:11, James 1:17, and Ephesians 1:3. Do something kind for three people today.

PRAYER
Father, forgive me for wanting out of a situation more than wanting to find You in it. Help me to remember that no adversity comes without Your permission. Increase my faith in You.

⊰BIRTH PAINS⊱
Winn Collier

In the birthing room where our son Wyatt entered the
world, my wife Miska held to her desire for a natural
birth, aided only by my uncertain encouragement and
the gentle massages of her *doula* (a birthing coach). As
Miska's contractions grew only a minute apart, the pain
intensified. Contrary to the zealous stories of natural
birth "love sessions" and moms "squealing with delight,"
this was no giddy affair. Giving birth is painful.

Mark records Jesus' allusion to the pain of birth. His
disciples asked how they would know when the end of
the age had come, inaugurating God's *ultimate* Kingdom
reign. Rather than answering directly, He revealed the
path God's plan would follow. Jesus said there would be
disturbing events—violent wars, chaos, and natural
disasters—which were simply the "beginning of birth
pains." These distress-filled days were necessary to birth
a kingdom, one that would be worth all the agony. The
passing affliction would introduce a far better day:
God's day.

This is a spiritual axiom: the work of God in our heart is
often birthed in pain. As much as I cringe to acknowl-
edge it, this will be true for our new son Wyatt. While
filled with delight over his entrance into the world, there
is also an undertone of sorrow. I fear, for I know the suffering world he enters. I fear for the pain I know will
greet him in this life—pain from which I can offer no
protection. But as much as I grieve, I also rejoice. Each

of us must face birthing pains if we are ever to move deeper into our calling.

These moments of agony connect us with our brokenness, and we see our need for a Savior. God may graciously wound us—as severe as it may be at times—to allow us to embrace the story of the Gospel. These passing wounds will give birth to something far better than a mere leisurely life: a person deeply connected with his God, intensely aware of his brokenness, and free to follow the path of God's design.

We cherish the absence of pain and do much to guard it. However, God seeks to birth in us something far more valuable than the absence of pain: the fruit of pain's deep soul-plowing. Without pain, we are unable to connect with the depth of our desperation for God. Without pain, we cannot embrace the wonder of the Gospel. Without pain, we cannot see the Kingdom of God *fully* birthed in our souls.

EVEN DEEPER
Study Romans 8:21-23 and Psalm 119:50, 75-77. Review the story of your life. Does your soul wince with pain at any point? Are you running from your pain or embracing it?

PRAYER
God, I sense I don't trust you. I don't trust that You are good even when I experience pain—in fact, that You are good *because* You allow pain. Help me to trust. Help me to follow, through pain, deeper into You.

As Christians, we can spot it a mile away. "Christian" rock, "Christian" rap, "Christian" pop. Re-packaged versions of our secular favorites, "Christian" stylings attempt to put a more meaningful face on the pop and progressive culture we love. But this face comes across as suspect; like I said, we can spot this stuff a mile away. And, we should ask ourselves, "What good is this face anyway?" Whether a secular or Christian veneer glosses the culture we love to consume, shouldn't we be looking deeper than this? Pop culture and progressive lifestyles might fuel our initial interests, but do they fuel our interior spirituality?

Here's the deal: we love fame, we love star-power, and if you rock, well, all the better. It's a simple fact of the twenty-first century. As Christians who've been entrenched in media culture nearly all our lives, we look to rockers and rappers, attempting to figure out how immersed we can get while still "defending the faith," staying true to our roots in Christ.

Our first stop? Christians gone public—secular culture is where we head. Let's be honest, who really flips to the DayStar network first? Some begrudgingly have to admit this fact. We'd like to say Christian rock is loved just the same, but it's not. That's why Jars of Clay, P.O.D., and other bands who've crossed the secular divide continually receive the praise and publicity.

The fact is, we check these bands out, hoping to pick up some tips. After all, they've been able to make the individual, internal relevance of Christ apparent in an external way that strikes a chord with the secular world. And isn't the secular world of media, entertainment, and culture where we really choose to live each day?

Popular culture serves, for many of us, as our weigh station in life. However, our choice to move in secular circles shouldn't translate to a dependency on others to bring Christ into this space. We can't expect the crossover success of our Christian favorites to buoy our individual notions of spiritual relevance. Just because U2 has found a way to externalize the Christianity that drives them at the core doesn't mean that we can simply look to their model and hope that they externalize Christ for us.

Making Christianity relevant within the pop-fueled circles we choose to live in is work that can never be done by grafting someone else's understanding of Christ onto our lives. Failing to take up this work as individuals means the beginning of "spiritual malaise."

This is a difficult concept to understand. Doesn't the success of Christian crossovers simply scream, "Hey you—this is how to be a culturally relevant Christian! See, I love God and I still found a way to become famous; I still thrive in the media culture we've grown to love"? Unfortunately, the answer is no. What crossover success should scream to you is, "Hey, I've learned to externalize what I was keeping inside the church, or myself, for so long. I was true to myself, and guess what? Others responded!" The simple fact is this: These bands have been able to externalize their internal faith across the traditional division between what is religious and what is secular. Furthermore, the externalization of feelings we hold within often solidifies our understanding of what we care about, what we're committed to.

Spiritual malaise is the opposite. We have no solidification of what we care about because we've never externalized it, put it out there; we've never looked at it outside the container of Christianity. Instead, we've always looked to others to "show us how," letting them do the work we so desperately need to be doing ourselves.

Finding a way to externalize our Christianity in secular space is one way to thwart spiritual malaise. We don't need to become rock stars, but we do need to quit segregating our lives into compartments, forever fixing our eyes upon the famous few who cross over (and away from) these segregated spaces. We need to let go of useless formulas for living a Christian life, i.e., worship band = externalizing *my* faith; secular space = watching Creed externalize *their* faith. Spiritual malaise forever shadows those of us who rely on rockers, and other artists, to give public props to God. Malaise follows those of us who pull our Christianity in and out of our pocket depending on the company we keep.

Simple honesty can cure this, though. If we can admit that the landscape we love is popular culture, defined by the pluralism we see and hear onscreen and onstage, then that is where we need to find our relevance—in the environment that fuels us, that we're passionate about being a part of. This doesn't mean we don't go to church and revolve in some "Christian circles," but a life lived across boundaries—one that rocks both religion and culture—is the life we need to be living.

Those who are lauded most for crossing the Christian/secular divide inspire us because they model this philosophy. These bands seem "real" because they revolve in "real" space, space that is varied and pluralistic. These bands rock us because they seem to have found a way to break from the partitioned practices of the Christian ghetto. From Ozzfest to the Grammys, there's no divide; Christianity is externalized right alongside all categories of content, all sensibilities of style.

Bands come and go, but we have to live with ourselves

forever. And we have to live inside the spaces we create for ourselves. The longer we depend on others to bring Christ into these spaces, the longer we ultimately pursue a life of "window gazing." By linking our sense of spiritual relevance to what we see modeled in the window, and by letting those models transcend the compartments we refuse to tear down, we ultimately window gaze in order to fit a mannequin: ourselves. To counter this sense of emptiness or spiritual malaise, don't shy away from externalizing what you know to be real for yourself upon the wider landscape you'd like to live in. You'll be surprised at what your passion will contribute toward an understanding of what you truly care about and believe. Like the stars you look to for reference and reassurance, you just might find that by doing this, you've made yourself "real" too.

GOD
OF
GREATNESS

❧THE STORY OF GOD❧
Winn Collier

Few things move us like a story. *Schindler's List* evoked repentant sorrow for the agony of Jewish suffering in a way no intellectual lecture on the evils of Nazism ever could. The pursuit of a dying father for his self-destructing son in the movie *Life as a House* opened up old wounds long forgotten.

Why do young boys don capes and scribble giant "S's" on their T-shirts? Why do little girls prance around the house in imaginary glass slippers? Stories. They move us, beckon us, capture us.

Madeleine L'Engle offered a glimpse behind this mystical power of story: "A story always tells us more than the mere words, and that is why we love to write it and to read it." The story invites us in to connect with a world that is here—and has always been here—but that we have unwittingly forgotten and discarded amid the incessantly ringing cell phone, the clamor at work, and the ceaseless social calendar. Story is missing, and thus our connection to the deeper parts of our heart is missing, too.

There is another, more fundamental reason why stories connect with our deepest places. God is the great Storyteller. Whenever Jesus wanted to get a point across, He crafted a story, or parable. However, as powerful as the storytelling ministry of Jesus was, God is the master of the story for a much grander reason. There really is only one narrative, one central story; and this tale flowed from the quill of God. God authored *the* story. He crafted the plot. He set the stage. He painted the setting. And He penciled Himself in as the central character.

This grand story is the Gospel. The hero is God. The villain is Evil and all of his terror. The cause for which the Hero fights is His glory…and His people. We have great reason to be drawn to story—because in the story we find our hope.

All stories—mine, yours, and every tale that has been told—are simply subplots, reflections back to that one grand story. They are chapters of the larger novel. In these smaller chapters, we catch glimpses of the glory of God, His redemptive story, and our joyful hope. For, as G.K. Chesterton rightly noted, "Every good story is simply a retelling of the Gospel."

EVEN DEEPER
Read Jesus' story in John 3:16 and 15:13. Then cozy up to your favorite classic novel. See how the story of God, the Gospel, is offered in its pages.

PRAYER
God, You move me deeply. Your words have challenged me, Your life has inspired me, and Your story captures me. Allow me to see today how I connect with the story You are still writing.

⊰NOTHING LEFT⊱
Jason Johns

"Because by one sacrifice he has made perfect forever those who are being made holy" (Hebrews 10:14).

There is nothing left to do.

I like the sound of that. My life is a maze of tasks and deadlines. Projects for work here, papers and tests for school there. There is grass to be mowed, a friend to see, family to care for. At the end of the day, I am exhausted, and yet I fall asleep thinking of things that I have to do tomorrow.

Hanging on the cross, Jesus did all that needed to be done. He finished the work of salvation once and for all. He has made us perfect. We are complete. We are whole.

There is nothing left to do.

Such an idea counters our western philosophy of accomplishment. Who are we without tasks to keep us occupied? Many Christians are tireless in their efforts for God, motivated both by an authentic desire to draw closer to Him and out of fear that God is never satisfied.

But it is finished. There is no sacrifice left for us to bring. Our efforts are not the issue. We are whole in Christ. Can we rest in His love?

There is nothing left to do.

Resting in Him is not a license to ignore the needs of others, to grow lazy, to shun the calling of God on our life. It is an invitation from a loving God to "seek first the Kingdom of God." We can rest and step into His Kingdom.

There is nothing left to do.

EVEN DEEPER
Consider Psalm 4:8 and Matthew 11:28-29. This week, take a look at your motivation for the way you live your life. Remembering that His sacrifice has made you complete, take an inventory of your days to discover where it is you are attempting to gain favor by your activity. Claim His promise of rest.

PRAYER
Jesus, thank You that there is nothing left for me to do. I want to rest in You. Teach me what it is to rest.

✥THE THRESHOLD OF GLORY✥
Stephen C. Baldwin

Christ's ascension is an often-neglected passage. It shouldn't be.

Theologians tell us that the disciples watched as Christ ascended to His throne until clouds obscured Him from their sight. He was taking the seat from which He exercises "all authority in heaven and on earth" (Matthew 28:18). What else was happening in the courts of heaven, invisible to our eyes? Much has not been revealed to us, but what we have been given can whet our appetite for heaven.

When the risen Jesus traversed the threshold that separates earth and heaven, He strode into the joy of His Father, went from the realm where He completed His work to the heavenly sanctuary. Victorious over Satan, having disarmed and despoiled him of a mighty host of captives given to Him by the Father, He ascended to His throne. He entered the presence of the Father, whose transcendent power, holiness, and mercy have been vindicated by His beloved Son and Champion, the Lion of Judah.

Perhaps in that moment, the countless fearsome angelic beings abased themselves in wordless awe, then rose to shout and shake the very stars with their praise!

As He entered heaven, in union with Him was a host, a nation, a vast new people as diverse as the manifold peoples of the earth, a palette of "living stones" for His unending praise, given to Him by the Father. Before the throne of God's grace, in heaven's sanctuary, we are represented by the Righteous One. There we have God's own Son, forevermore bearing the wounds He received to make atonement for us.

There before our Father He is not ashamed to call us His brethren. There He rules over the entire universe for the high glory of God and the good of His beloved. From there He prays for us and always sends us aid. He is ever attentive to our prayers, holding our tears and sufferings more precious than the radiance of His halls. There the Lord and King of Glory reigns for His own until all of His (and our) enemies will be made His footstool, until death itself dies and unending, unabated ages of joy ensue.

Today take great strength, comfort, and joy in the grace that now flows to us from the Lord Jesus, the ascended King of heaven and earth.

EVEN DEEPER
Read Exodus 15:10-12. Carve out time to be alone. Get on your knees. You are bowing before the throne of the Ascended One. Pour your heart out to Him.

PRAYER
Ascended One, You are mighty. You reign. You are worthy of worship. You are worthy of all. I kneel as Your servant. Flow Your grace toward me.

⊰A PSALM⊱
Alecia Stephens

I praise you, Lord God, that You are the great Artist and that creation is Your canvas. As a painter steps back and sighs in contentment at his finished work, so You delight in the beauty You have created by Your good pleasure.

I see how You have carved the valleys out of mountains like a sculptor. Each crevice and cliff has a place in your grand design, and as I look down upon Your work, I see that each crevice and cliff creates a breathless scene. Every waterfall that flows down from the mountains replenishes Your work. I stand at the bottom of the rushing waters and feel the cool mist upon my face. I see dozens of rainbows before the falls and agree that Your creation is good.

I stand at the base of the granite peaks, in wonder of their mass. I grow aware of how small I am compared to the Creator and Artist. I wonder how You can ever notice me in the vastness of Your work?

I hear the music You make in the roar of the waterfalls, in the bird's song, in the hush of the breeze through the green meadows, and most of all in the silence.

I love the colors of the flowers You created. Many artists try to capture the hues You have mixed, but none compare with Your design. Your have saved your most beautiful colors for the sunset, painting the gray, rocky peaks in their shades.

I believe You greatly rejoice in bathing your creation with the light of the moon. You take pleasure in my gaping over the beauty. I know You have created the multitude of stars, hanging them in place.

I see this art and am drawn to the Artist. It is He who formed the masterpiece, and it is He who holds it together. And I cannot help but praise the Creator.

EVEN DEEPER
Revisit the account of creation in Genesis 1, 2. Take some time to go to the mountains, the beach, or even a park in your town, and spend time praising God for His creation.

PRAYER
I thank You, Lord, that Your beauty is all around me. Help me to see the works of Your hand.

❧MAGNIFICENT MONOTONY❧
Jeremy Klaszus

Wake up. Eat. Work. Sleep. Do it all over again tomorrow. And the next day. And the next.

Is it possible to live intimately with God when stuck in the often dreaded routine of everyday life? Could God have valuable lessons to teach us through our monotonous routines? He does, but unfortunately, we are often too busy wishing for what we don't have to notice. We look at others—Bible characters, friends, or missionaries—and think how much opportunity God has given them to be salt and light to the world. We look enviously at all of their opportunities and discard our own.

We are tempted to think that simply because we do the same thing every day, God renders us ineffective. The opposite is true. The reality is that *we* render *Him* ineffective because we get bored of our routine. We grow weary of repetition. But our Father doesn't, and rather than being bored with the monotony, He may be the designer of it.

G.K. Chesterton explained this idea brilliantly: "Perhaps God is strong enough to exult in monotony. It is possible that God says every morning, 'Do it again' to the sun; and every evening, 'Do it again' to the moon...The repetition in Nature may not be a mere recurrence; it may be a theatrical encore."

We have all heard that we "can do all things through Christ" (Philippians 4:13 KJV), but do we believe this strength is strong enough to move us to "do it again" when we wake in the morning, fresh for the challenge of yet another day? Can we see our life as more than an audio book locked on repeat?

I need not look far for strength each day—I only need to look out my window. For even as I hear the dreaded buzz of my alarm clock, I can see that this morning, God has not been idle. He has done one more time what he has done millions of times: once again, He has instructed the sun to rise, the wind to blow, and the birds to sing. And if He can do that millions of times over, surely I can face the day ahead with Him. Together we can delight in the magnificence of monotony.

EVEN DEEPER
Meditate on Galatians 6:9. Think about which part of your week is the most monotonous. What have you come to dread? How can you see God's hand in those moments?

PRAYER
God of each moment, I want to see my time as You see it—each minute crafted by You, each hour an opportunity to live out the life You offer.

⊰LIVING DANGEROUSLY⊱
Tom Mulnix

In *Dangerous Wonder*, Michael Yaconelli writes, "Remember the thrill of thinking you could fly, the adventure of going places in your imagination, the joy and abandon of running and jumping and playing hard—without worrying about what might happen?"

Some of us remember what it's like to be a child. Fearless wonder—some call it innocence. It's the discovery of something new, the abandonment of our whole selves to living life. Somewhere along the path to adulthood, things change. We're taught to "grow up." Some behaviors just aren't acceptable when you get older.

Stop crying. Quit goofing off. You're laughing too loud. Sit still. Emotions are considered foolishness, and before you know it, we become the adult who doesn't display passion about anything. We are lost.

I think we sell out with this dignified behavior. I think we miss the God-intended joy of living life.

One of the Hebrew words for praise is *halal*. It means to celebrate, to rave, and to act foolishly. Foolish actions are acceptable to God. He loves them; they're heartfelt.

Life is meant to be enjoyed. Our emotions are meant to be explored. We are designed to live with reckless wonder. Our emotions and feelings are a vital part of who we are. I have determined that I will show my passion. Hug my friends. Giggle with my kids. Kiss my wife. Let them call me foolish.

What about you? Are you ready to live dangerously?

EVEN DEEPER
Read how David lost his inhibitions in 2 Samuel 6:12-15. Lose a little dignity this week. Rediscover that feeling of getting lost in the moment without worrying about what other people think. Dance in the rain with the one you love. Throw your head back and act foolishly in worship at church. I dare you.

PRAYER
God, help me to be honest with myself and with others. Let others see in me a zeal for life and all it has to offer. Help me to live dangerously.

❧GOD AROUND ME❧
Malcolm Johnson

Ali and I live in a small town on the west coast of Canada, a place blessed by rolling surf and surrounded by coastal rainforests. It was early summer, and the wind had been blowing onshore all day. But late in the evening, the winds died, and we drove south for the day's last wave check.

Running down the beach path, we were excited by glassed-off, peeling waves and the sky turning strange hues of pink, purple, and gold. We threw on our wet-suits, grabbed our boards, and paddled into the surf.

We slid in and out of the small but perfect waves, enjoying the sunset. The black silhouette of the Humpback Mountains and the huge Sitka spruce trees filled the dusk sky. A pack of sea lions joined us, poking their heads up to look at us. They body-surfed the waves with an aplomb we humans could never match.

That evening, the surf session was pure West Coast goodness, and during it, I reflected on God's request, "Be still and know that I am God" (Psalm 46:10). I sat on my board, feeling the swell that had come from thousands of miles away, and thought, "This is how God moves around me."

These are the best times with God. Times when you can be still, slow down, and allow yourself to simply be.

Times when you can rediscover your place in God and in the world, enjoying creation singing His praise. And, like the sea lions body-surfing the waves, times when you can enter into the flow and take simple joy in the graces that roll in, waves from the great ocean that is our deep and fathomless God.

Our God is pervasive, powerful, and unrestrained in His blessings. There is no end to where you can see Him if you open your eyes and your heart, if you surrender and are receptive.

EVEN DEEPER
Meditate on Psalm 66:4-6, then find a place to relax. Watch a sunset. Sit in front of the ocean. Find a natural place where God's presence is unmistakable. And then, do nothing. Just let yourself be in the knowledge that God is there.

PRAYER
Our Father, You are here. Your presence moves around me, and Your beauty surrounds me. Let me find You where I seek You; let me see You in places I never have before. Let me lose myself in You.

Looking for the Real Thing
John M. De Marco

Jamal works the phones by night as a telemarketer. By day, he's hanging with the hip-hop community of South Florida, trying to make things happen as a producer and musician. The twenty-four year old wants to sing about the stuff of real life, the true feelings that flow out when you take off the mask. People are hungry to be heard for how they really see life, Jamal believes.

He's listening to DMX. "He's a very influential artist on the level of being real about certain things in life, things that go on every day," Jamal said. "It definitely inspires me in several ways to keep going. There's gonna be dark days and sunshine days. We've got to weather the dark days in order to see the sunshine days."

In DMX, Jamal relates to an artist who captures the paradox of living in a violent world that will chew you up if you let down your guard—yet a life where you get stronger by yielding yourself to a greater power. "I come to you hungry and tired/You give food and let me sleep/I come to you weak/You give strength and that's deep," the artist belts in "Prayer."

Hardcore bands help twenty-seven-year-old Karyn, who works in advertising and sales in northeast Ohio, process the events of her life. Tracy Chapman inspires and comforts her with stories of struggle and perseverance. And the movie *Alive*, a true account of a soccer team that survived a plane crash and lived out of the wreckage for fifty days, "comes in handy when [she] think[s] life is really crummy."

Kim, twenty-three, a contract scheduler in Texas, connects to Madonna's ongoing search for contentment and the lyrics and voice of Sarah McLachlan. "One of her [McLachlan's] most popular songs is about having people accept you for everything you are, including all of the ugliness inside of you," she said. "This strikes a chord with me because this is definitely a stage I am in, having my co-workers, friends, and family accept me as an adult."

She also resonates with the movie *Fight Club* and its unnerving expressions of male anger, relating to one film character's insight that "the things you own end up owning you. It's only after you've lost everything that you're free to do anything." It's freedom from being defined by what you have or do—another rare gem worth pocketing.

On many occasions, it seems that pop culture is an end in itself, entertainment for entertainment's sake. Some would say there's no value to be found across its image-driven, overly commercialized landscape. However, pop for its own sake may be an illusion. As shallow as something may seem, there is a connection being made. Emotion is touching emotion. Feeling is reaching out to feeling. Spirit is resonating with spirit.

People of the eighteen to thirty-four-year-old cluster in our society are connecting with musicians, films, television programming, and books that embrace our daily struggles and seek to provide perspective and purpose in the midst of it all. Amid the sheer thrill of entertainment and escape, a search is at hand, a quest for hearing and being heard, for achieving fulfillment and understanding—for surviving—in a rapidly changing and often depersonalizing global culture.

And this search is spiritual in nature. Lauryn Hill told MTV News of the "inner peace" she felt after the two-year sabbatical she took following the release of *The Miseducation of Lauryn Hill*. She spent the time intensely studying Scripture. Instead of music or fame, she now looks to something or Someone bigger for fulfillment. So does most of our generation, it seems. We want power for living a life that matters. This vibrant spirituality flourishing among our generation doesn't necessarily want to be confined to organized religion or dogmatic truth.

It longs to be spontaneous, malleable, expressed through the senses, accepted for its diversity. It embraces prayer, sees a clear line of demarcation between right and wrong and hinges on personal responsibility. And it is by and large being fed by the gatekeepers of the pop culture universe rather than by the doctrinal pulpits of America.

"I really don't answer to anyone else. I know that I am responsible for my actions, and that helps me to want to be more spiritual," said Krista, a twenty-year-old college student. "I just disagree with the commercialization attached to spirituality in today's society. We are so far away from the true meaning of religion, we can't even see it anymore."

Dave, a thirty-four-year-old attorney, also doesn't derive his spirituality from the mainstream church. "If I pray every morning and remember to do God's will through-out the day, I feel good," he said.

It is a God-laden world, and people are hungry to push back the layers that obscure a taste of His reality. The pop culture preachers are with you. Genre-bending P.O.D. proclaim they feel "so alive, for the very first time," giving listeners a burst of energy that's positive and edgy and scary and intriguing all at the same moment. And we still adore U2 with all its reinvention and are awed by Bono's relentless endeavors through music and action to make this world a place where peace, justice, and love reign above all. These are issues that matter to us deeply. These artists are nourishing our souls and inspiring us to make a difference.

We resonate strongly with movies such as *Pay It Forward*, with its emphasis on kindness toward strangers, and *From Hell* with its reminder of the ever-dangling choice we face between good and evil. The cult hit *Unbreakable* speaks to our own search for someone whose attributes are the polar opposite of our acknowledged frailties, that one "unbreakable" person. As rationale, creative beings, we grapple with issues such as life and death, alternative lifestyles and subsequent guilt, the ever-availability of self-destructive behaviors, and balancing our families and vocations—no wonder HBO's "Six Feet Under" and "The Sopranos" and Cinemax's "Soul Food" grab a lot of our cathode ray investments.

"*Traffic* is a film that really struck a chord with me (every pun intended)," said Charles, a thirty-two-year-old Texas-based musician. "I, too, came from an unfortunate upbringing and struggled with the peril of drugs within my family. I think one of the problems we have in our society today is the lack of communication between parents and their children. A lot of parents are in denial and think their child is perfect and would never hang out with the wrong crowd." Facing the true predicaments that impact us as civilized people—it's the struggle that is under-girded by our spiritual bedrock.

Some of us are looking for that under-girding in America's bookstores, where Deepak Chopra wants to make God accessible to us. *Fight Club* and *Choke* author Chuck Palahniuk is seeking to emphasize that even the most dysfunctional among us have the need for true community. Ayn Rand reminds us of the importance of the decisions that we make, as our society's pressure to have one's act together grows more immense. Self-help books such as the *Don't Sweat* series keep finding their way onto our desks. It all reads like an endless quest for improvement, awareness, understanding, for not living a life that is wasted and without meaning. It gets exhausting.

"Man is constantly searching for answers to questions," said thirty-four-year-old Bryan, a South Carolina pediatrician. "He is constantly pursuing his *raison d'etre*, or reason to be. I think God is his definition of the unexplained entity that gave us our reason to be. He exists as we see Him to exist."

Interestingly, we're also making modern worship music a viable genre at Wal-Mart and Best Buy. There's something authentic about this particular brand of unapologetic worship that intrigues us. And what's even more intriguing is the fact that, given our generation's strong resistance toward having its spirituality boxed in or defined, this genre boldly places its trust in the one person who many feel sheds light and truth upon spirituality itself—Jesus.

Only Jesus knew whether He was the Son of God, said Bryan, who refers to Christ as a "great teacher and scholar." But is there more to this Jesus character than just great teachings? Amid all of this earthy, raw spirituality and the delicious *a la carte* menu available for its nourishment, the pieces so often seem to elude a cohesive glue, a big picture focus and foundation that makes sense of—and gives a satisfying conclusion to—all of the searching. We can still feel so fragmented—as though our spirituality, vocation, and relationships only mesh together into holistic living part of the time. Our accumulated knowledge of things practical and spiritual can often fail to produce genuine power for becoming the person we want to be.

Where is the lasting strength behind the acknowledgement that Lauryn Hill finally feels, the consistent sense of "feeling alive" that P.O.D. shouts? Where can we encounter the "unbreakable" person who must be out there somewhere, who can tell us the secret for how we also might bend without breaking? Is there truly a fulfilling community that the angst-ridden souls of *Fight Club* and *Choke* are desperately seeking?

It can be hard to find this measure of fellowship or even perceive that it actually exists. "I have always just felt like a fish out of water (in the church), and am most comfortable honoring God in my own private way," said Paige, a twenty-nine-year-old corporate trainer in Georgia. So if Jesus' own "people" can make us feel out of place, why even try the corporate worship thing?

Jesus maintained that His very life at work in frail, imperfect people creates the authentic community that much of organized religion is unable to foster because of its stubborn unwillingness to live out His message. His life, it seems, is our power to be a survivor. To be unbreakable.

The search demands persistence and tolerance. "I was getting a little agnostic for awhile there, until I recently found the church I'm currently going to," Karyn said. "I see people who attend this church, and the only way I can describe them is they're full of God ... You can see it when they sing, when they speak, in their faces when they listen, and in their children. It's really rather amazing, and I'm striving to achieve that kind of relationship."

Authentic community that worships the authentic God is doable. It's possible. It's somewhere in our midst if we'll keep looking with eyes to find. It's buildable through our efforts—or through yielding to that greater power. We too can become "full of God," at last filling the empty space that remains inside despite the non-stop consumption of all our culture has to offer.

"I'm not a fan of organized religion as it is today," said Nini, a twenty-five-year-old Washington, D.C.-based consultant. "However, I am in favor of groups of people coming together and sharing with one another from the Bible. I believe as a Christian I need that support I can only get from other people who share similar interests." Paternalistic editors not withstanding, the recorded words of Christ ring true to our tangled longings without exception. They slowly reveal how all other philosophies are bright-to-pale imitations. As we take that leap from word to experience, and dare to ask Jesus in concrete ways to prove that He's as alive and eternal as He says he is, the pieces finally come together and the restlessness bleeds into power that fosters inner peace.

He's not calling us to divorce our pop culture, as the church often insists, but to view all that we embrace or reject in light of His truth. It's not elitist or divisive to proclaim Him as the One, because His character, power and love are the very definition of truth and goodness. There's no shame in adoring Him.

Jesus makes sense. He makes sense of why we love the things we love. He makes sense of why we look at relationships, politics, and the world the way we do. The pain inflicted by His lukewarm followers and the way we sometimes rationalize have caused many of us to miss out on a relationship that makes sense of life's big questions and provides the lasting joy that otherwise slips between the fragments.

Jesus is accessible. He's timelessly relevant. And in the midst of the marketing machines of the pop culture universe, He is patiently and lovingly speaking to each of us.

FEAR WITHOUT FRIGHT
Faith Hopler

It's difficult to connect to the notion that we were made by an awful God, total in His power and omniscience. It's difficult to grasp this portion of God's character, especially in a modern world that gives us the illusion of control over nature and encourages an attitude of invincibility.

But the fear of God is a common theme in Scripture. Proverbs 9:10 tells us, "The Fear of the Lord is the beginning of wisdom." Should we meditate on the reality that God could infect us with cancer, or blow away our possessions in a freak tornado? Do we fear a God who holds our lives in an iron clutch?

It's confusing. When a biblical character encounters God's presence, they're regularly told, "Don't be afraid!" Why are we told both to fear *and* to not be afraid?

This apparent contradiction unravels in the conclusion of the same proverb: "The knowledge of the Holy One is understanding." As we come to deeply know God, we relinquish the false masks we have laid over His image and commit ourselves to His true character. We are then able to face the reality that we are slavishly committed to having a God we can fully comprehend.

A.W. Tozer said, "We want a God we can in some measure control. We need the feeling of security that comes from knowing what God is like … A *proper* fear of God is a solemn, reverent respect based on His true character."

His varying attributes combine to form a perfect whole. When the awful power of God is set against His intense love, it can seem like another paradox in His nature. But Psalm 84:3 says, "Even the sparrow has found a home, and the swallow a nest for herself, where she may have her young—a place near your altar, O Lord Almighty, my King and my God!" Even the birds long to come close to the security and tenderness of God.

This tender protection is possible because God is King, powerful beyond all. The awesome strength of God allows Him to love us perfectly. Together, these two divine traits—strength and love—create a dimension where we can fear, yet not be afraid.

EVEN DEEPER
Consider Psalm 89:6-8 and Revelation 19:4-6. What images and emotions come to mind when you hear the phrase, "the fear of God"? Is there something unhealthy there? Ask God to reveal to you the comfort that comes in fearing Him.

PRAYER
God, at times I am afraid of You. At times, I dismiss You. I want neither. Move me to embrace You in holy awe.

⊰DRAWING CLOSE⊱
Derek MacLeod

In our quest for efficiency, we punch out e-mails quickly
to friends and colleagues. Avoiding the words that would
take too long to spell, we write in an abrupt, brisk fashion. At times I find myself applying this same "quick, get
it over and done with" attitude to my time with God.

I recently felt the effects of my briskness with God. I was
distant in my prayer time, scattered in my attempts to
worship. Prayer was more of a checklist than a conversa-
tion. Pondering over my plight, I realized the unthink-
able: I was ignoring God.

We often think of God as "detached." He's over there,
and we're over here. We are mistaken. God is with us.
He is around us. He covers us. He aches when we ignore
Him, too busy for our God. Yet He remains faithful. He
is just, jealous, angry, compassionate, and merciful. He
longs for us, our companionship, our fellowship. He
longs for our love.

We can't simply turn God on and off. We can't ignore
Him and then expect to experience His nearness whenever we feel the urge. All relationships in the human
dimension require love, care, and attention. They require
time. Relationships in the spiritual dimension are no
different. God is near. God is ready. God is waiting.

"Because of the Lord's great love we are not consumed, for his compassions never fail. They are new every morning; great is your faithfulness. I say to myself, 'The Lord is my portion; therefore I will wait for him'" (Lamentations 3:22-24).

The Lord waits for our unending worship. Sit down with Him. Go for a walk with Him; listen to Him. Take your relationship deeper and develop a treasured closeness to your Maker.

EVEN DEEPER
James 4:8 says, "Come near to God and he will come near to you." Find a place where you can meet God and set aside time solely for that purpose. God will meet with you.

PRAYER
Lord, it amazes me that You want to spend time with me. Forgive me for ignoring You. Place in my heart an eagerness to meet You and enjoy Your glorious presence.

⊰THE BEAUTY WITHIN⊱
Kyle Crouch

History is dotted with the fallibility of man. We are a people marred by scars from centuries of transgressions. Yet God considers us beautiful. Doesn't this contradict the definition of beauty? Isn't beauty flawless and pleasing to the senses?

In light of the mass of humanity's depravity—wars, evil schemes, and dishonest pursuits, how are we still considered beautiful by a God of perfection? We are beautiful because our mere existence reflects God's glory and joy.

We are able to feel, reason, and love. But love is a choice, and we are given the freedom to choose whether or not we will love in return. We determine to what measure we will reflect the beauty God has placed within us. Our bodies are only vessels carrying this infinite, eternal beauty of God. We must surrender our vessel to display the wonder it was designed to offer the world.

The mask of flesh covering our bodies is not the true depth of our beauty. It goes deeper, waiting to be released.

This release will happen if we are consumed with God. His thoughts become our thoughts. His ways become our ways. We are no longer our own; we are part of a larger composition, a body of people that is more than our individual existence. Yet how can we be absorbed by this larger composition and still maintain our unique inner beauty?

C.S. Lewis said it well in his book *Mere Christianity*: "Some people think that after this life, or perhaps after several lives, human souls will be 'absorbed' into God... It is only the Christians who have any idea of how human souls can be taken into the life of God and remain themselves—in fact, be very much more themselves than they were before."

So, by being taken into God, we find the release of the beauty we were created to display. It is a wonder, this beauty within.

EVEN DEEPER
Read Psalm 149:4 and Hebrews 13:15-16. What of God's beauty are you offering the world? Give a smile, a story, or a hug away today.

PRAYER
Great God, I want to be taken into You. I want to release Your beauty to the world. Absorb me.

≈ALL DAY≈
Winn Collier

Dawn. Awake. Crisp. Air. Rested. Birds. Chirp. Dew.
Alive. Dog. Out. Run. Newspaper. Coffee. Shower. Sing.
Pray. Sing. Shave. Nick. Bagel. Oranges. Wheaties.
Kiss. Kids. Lunchboxes. Kiss. School. Briefcase.
Commute. Radio. News. Noise. Honk. Reports.
Meetings. Coffee. Spill. Laugh. Argue. Create. Confront.
Joke. Appointment. Lunch. Sandwich. Salad. Pie. No.
Fruit. Office.

Midday. Phone. Conference. Call. Scribble. E-mail.
Fax. Pager. Deadline. Wired. Wireless. Headset. Pace.
Wrangle. Buy. Sell. Trade. Tylenol. Interrupt. Call.
Home. Smile. Love. Truth. Good. God. Commute.
Store. Forget. Return. Store. Traffic. Radio. News. Noise.
Horn. Home. Kids. Run. Jump. Play. Wrestle. Laugh.
Remember.

Dusk. Crickets. Chirp. Sky. Orange. Breeze. Streetlights.
Flicker. Dinner. Family. Laugh. Highchair. Spill. Laugh.
Mop. Ice Cream. Yes. Chocolate. Vanilla. Strawberry.
Mom. Dad. Walk. Twilight. Talk. Hands. Share. Laugh.
Remember. Kids. Bed. Up. Bed. Drink. Bed. Monsters.
Bed. Hushed. Quiet. Kisses. Rest. Good. God. Good.

"From the rising of the sun to its setting, the name of
the Lord is to be praised" (Psalm 113:3 NAS).

EVEN DEEPER

Write a few words that describe the flow of your day. How can these lead you to worship God? Study Psalm 113:3.

PRAYER

God of the rising and the setting sun, I want to experience you in the midst of the day, throughout it, and intertwined with it. Don't allow me to be content to just give you portions of it. I want all of You in all of me.

⊰IMAGINE THAT⊱
Steve Stockman

Jesus came to live among us, imagining and inspiring His followers to imagine. Imagine a son who throws his father's inheritance away in hedonistic over-indulgence coming home and getting a party thrown for him. Imagine a world where the workers who work for the last ten minutes get the same wage as those who worked all day. Imagine where the poor are blessed, where the mourners are comforted, where God's kingdom comes on earth as it is in heaven. Imagine that.

But do we? Missing from our modern church life is a wild imagining. Before God made, He imagined. Before we are going to make an impression, we need to imagine. We have become suspicious and fearful of this bold imagination, particularly in evangelicalism. The scientific ways of modernity have sneaked into our theologically rigid and behaviorally legalistic church: "This is how we do things."

The first thing we learn about God in Scripture is He imagined and created. All we know about who we are is that we are made in His image. We are like God, imaginers and artists. To follow Jesus is to begin to ask, what will the kingdom of God look like if it comes onto the streets of our country as it is in heaven? What would that mean for our churches? What would that mean for us in our use of money and time? How would it influence our relations with the poor? What would it mean in our relationships with the other side of our political divide? Could we imagine a hug there? Imagine that as a sign of the kingdom coming across the world's television sets.

My four-year-old daughter is already asking how to color inside the lines. Already her imagination is being oppressed and confined. I pray for her, as well as for you and me, that we would let our imaginations go mad, smash the lines to pieces and shimmy and shake this world on its head, so we might bring the provocative, agitating, yet gloriously beautiful wildness of God to the streets. Imagine that!

EVEN DEEPER
Meditate on Ephesians 3:20. Feed your child-like imagination. Go to the zoo. Grab a coloring book. Watch a cartoon. Explore the woods. Give someone you dislike a hug.

PRAYER
Creator God, help me to see the wonder of Your hands, the wonder You have created in me. Help me to see the world as it can be, Your Kingdom on earth as it is in Heaven.

⊰A GRACE OF WORSHIP⊱
Faith Hopler

"I often think of the set pieces of liturgy as certain words which people have successfully addressed to God without their getting killed. In the high churches they saunter through the liturgy like Mohawks along a strand of scaffolding who have long since forgotten their danger. If God were to blast such a service to bits, the congregation would be, I believe, genuinely shocked. But in the low churches you expect it any minute. This is the beginning of wisdom." (Annie Dillard, *Holy the Firm*).

The church service I attend on Sunday mornings is a picture of grace to me. We meet in a movie theater. Every Sunday it's a challenge to transform somewhere people go for entertainment into a place of community and worship. There aren't any Scripture banners. The sound system has its moments, and the Sunday School classes meet in the halls and in a party room. But somehow, every Sunday, people worship the living God of the universe. Children learn about the Bible and about Jesus who loves them. The pastors teach energetically, offering their wisdom from learning and experience. Somehow it all comes together. And no one gets blasted to bits.

The grace of God was seen when Jesus said to the woman by the well, "Believe me, a time is coming when you will worship the Father neither on this mountain nor in Jerusalem" (John 4:21). Jesus freed us to worship Him in all places, at all times, with the Spirit in our hearts and the truth on our lips. Even in the most secular of places, like a theater. Even in the most hazardous of times, like an early Sunday morning when I'm groggy and don't know what might come out of my mouth. But during those times and in those places we cannot forget who we worship because it's only by the grace of God we're there.

He is attentive to us, and we are attentive to Him. We hang on every word He might speak because we are acutely aware that only His grace could have brought each of us to this most unlikely place, with this holy body of rather normal people.

EVEN DEEPER
Read John 4:23-24. Ponder how you approach your worship of God. Is it bound to a place or a time? Step out. Worship God somewhere that you wouldn't have thought to previously.

PRAYER
God, I want to see Your grace in all time and in all space. You are here. Help me to see it.

⊰SHADOW OF THE TRUTH⊱
Benjamin Esposito

The film *Moulin Rouge* tells an enlightening story of the so-called "bohemian" ideals of truth, beauty, freedom, and love. The dreamers, artists, and prophets of our world often live lives of pretense. It seems that those who see more clearly often give up hope in the possibility that truth can be reached in daily reality. Reacting to this hopelessness, they spend their days searching for the elusive transcendent moment. In doing so, however, they unwittingly compromise the ideals they so passionately espouse.

The truth reached in a theatrical production is only a shadow of the truth, as each player is a pretender, acting out the life of another. The truth offered in a musical composition emerges as the music reaches its climax, where reality drops away and both performer and audience are swept to a far-off place. These are only fleeting shadows of reality, a hint of something greater. They are vain attempts to connect with that for which man was made.

In our postmodern age, truth has been confused and cheapened. In such an age, it is easy to give up hope in ultimate truth. Yet Jesus Christ said, "I am the way and the truth and the life" (John 14:6). Jesus didn't only speak the truth; He *is* the truth. And it is this truth that invites us to intimacy, to experience the reality of true connection with Him. While many passionate seekers settle for a mere shadow of truth, the opportunity is here to follow and worship the One who is truth.

When Jesus walked on the earth, He challenged a group of followers to delve into the depths of truth. He challenged them to delve into Him. Jesus incarnated truth,
and He asked them to do the same, to move from believing His words to *living* them. Only then would they find truth. Only then would they surrender their shadows for the real thing.

EVEN DEEPER
Read John 8:31-36. This week, meditate on the metaphor of shadows. Are you living in the shadow of truth, or are you delving into the True One?

PRAYER
Holy Spirit, Jesus called You the spirit of truth and said You would lead and guide me into all truth. Forgive me for the ways I've settled for shadows of truth, and help me instead to pursue Jesus Christ.

ᗄA YEARNING FOR GLORYᗄ
Winn Collier

Idolaters have overrun the land. Pagans mock Israel's
God. Barely hanging on, a beleaguered people teeter on
the jagged edge of despair. Vicious enemies, a blood-
thirsty lot, crouch on Israel's borders. The land empties
of hope. God does nothing.

God's people are desperate for their God to move. They
offer an earnest, desperate plea. A wounded people with
nothing to lose, they ask God for what they truly want,
their deepest desire: God's glory. "Not to us, O Lord, not
to us, but to your name be the glory" (Psalm 115:1).
This is not a theological ideal or a religious platitude.
This is a cry of the heart.

Their request for God's glory was not simply a means to
something else they wanted more, like a child stuffing
down his broccoli so he can get to the chocolate cake.
They weren't saying, "God, bring glory to yourself so we
can get what we want." They were pleading, "God, bring
all the glory to yourself—*this* is what we crave."

How could God's glory be their deepest longing, especially at a time like this? Israel had no problem asking
God for many other things. Regularly, they asked God
for rain, the destruction of their enemies, large broods of
kids, bountiful harvest, and wisdom. Yet in this critical
moment they craved God's glory more than victory,
more than power, even more than safety.

Israel had staked everything on God. Their existence centered on the conviction that Yahweh was *their God*. God was their identity. They bore His name, and their created purpose offered them their most passion-filled joy: the glory of their King. Worship was their highest aim.

Israel knew God as more than the giver of "good stuff." For them, pleasure was not simply the sum of what God provided. Pleasure was God Himself. God was their joy, their hope, their Father, their life. If God did not tailor everything to His glory alone, then God was not who He said He was, their existence was meaningless, and ultimate pleasure was lost.

So, they begged God to guard His glory. In this, Israel was asking for pure, unadulterated pleasure—pleasure that can only come from a grand God. Are we so bold? Do we know what it is to yearn for deep pleasure in the glory of God?

EVEN DEEPER
Read Psalm 16:11 and 84:2 and Matthew 6:19-21. Reflect on the patterns of your life. What is it you yearn for? Are you experiencing the deep pleasure connected to seeking after God's glory?

PRAYER
We join with the cry of David, "Not to us, O Lord, not to us, but to Your name be the glory."

AUTHOR INDEX

BLOOD
ROSES

Francesca Lia Block

BLOOD
ROSES

JOANNA COTLER BOOKS

An Imprint of HarperCollins*Publishers*

HARPER TEEN

"Blood Roses" was originally published in *Firebirds Rising:
An Anthology of Original Science Fiction and Fantasy*,
edited by Sharyn November (Firebird, 2006).

Library of Congress Cataloging-in-Publication Data
Block, Francesca Lia.
Blood roses / Francesca Lia Block. — 1st ed.
    p.   cm.
Summary: A collection of magic realist stories of transforma-
tion.
    "'Blood Roses' is reprinted from *Firebirds Rising: An Anthology
of Original Science Fiction and Fantasy*, published in 2006 by
Firebird, an imprint of Penguin Group (USA) Inc."—Copyright
p.
    Contents: Blood roses — Giant — My haunted house — My
boyfriend is an alien — Horses are a girl's best friend — Skin art
— My mother the vampire — Wounds and wings — Changelings.
    ISBN 978-0-06-076384-8 (trade bdg.) — ISBN 978-0-06-
076385-5 (lib. bdg.)
    1. Short stories, American. 2. Supernatural—Juvenile fic-
tion. [1. Short stories. 2. Supernatural—Fiction.] I. Title.
PZ7.B61945Blo 2008   2007029564
[Fic]—dc22   CIP
                                                 AC

Typography by Carla Weise
1 2 3 4 5 6 7 8 9 10
❖
First Edition

For all of you...
willing to transform

Also by Francesca Lia Block

Weetzie Bat
Cherokee Bat and the Goat Guys
Missing Angel Juan
Girl Goddess #9: Nine Stories
The Hanged Man
Dangerous Angels: The Weetzie Bat Books
I Was a Teenage Fairy
Violet & Claire
The Rose and The Beast
Echo
Guarding the Moon
Wasteland
Goat Girls: Two Weetzie Bat Books
Beautiful Boys: Two Weetzie Bat Books
Necklace of Kisses
Psyche in a Dress

BLOOD
ROSES

Contents

Blood Roses

$\mathcal{E}$very day, Lucy and Rosie searched for the blood roses in their canyon. They found eucalyptus and poison oak, evening primrose and oleander but never the glow-in-the-dark red, smoke-scented flowers with sharp thorns that traced poetry onto your flesh.

"You only see them if you die," Lucy said, but Rosie just smiled so that the small row of pearls in her mouth showed.

Still, the hairs stood up on both their fore-arms and napes that evening, turning them to furry faunesses for a moment as they sat watching the sunset from their secret grotto in the heart of the canyon. The air smelled of exhaust fumes and decaying leaves. The sky was streaked with smog and you could hear the sound of cars and one siren but that world felt very far away.

Here, the girls turned doll-size, wove nests out of twigs to sleep in the eucalyptus branches, collected morning dew in leaves and dined on dark purple berries that stained their mouths and hands.

"We'd better get home," Lucy said, brushing the dirt off her jeans.

They would have stayed here all night in spite of the dangers—snakes, coyote, rapists,

goblins. It was better than the apartment made of tears where their mother had taken them when she left their father.

Their mother said their father was an alcoholic and a sex addict but all Lucy remembered was the sandpaper roughness of his chin, like the father in her baby book *Pat the Bunny*, when he hugged her and Rosie in his arms at the same time. He had hair of blackbird feathers and his eyes were green semiprecious stones.

Lucy and Rosie loved Emerson Solo because like their father he was beautiful, dangerous and unattainable. Especially now. Emerson Solo, twenty-seven, had stabbed himself to death in the heart last month.

You really had to want to die to be successful at that, their mother said before she confiscated all their Solo CDs and posters. Lucy understood why she'd done it. But still she wanted to look at his face and hear his voice again. For some reason he comforted her, even now. Was it because he had escaped?

≈

Lucy and Rosie were in the music store looking through the Emerson Solo discs. There was the one with the black bird on the cover called *For Sorrow* and the one called *The White Room*. There was a rumor that the white room was supposed to be death. The store was all out of *Collected* with the photo of Emerson Solo holding a bouquet of wildflowers with their dirty roots dragging down out of his hands.

A man was standing across the aisle from them and when Lucy looked up he smiled. He was young and handsome with fair hair, a strong chin.

"You like him?" he asked.

Rosie said, "Oh, yes! Our mom threw out all his CDs. We just come and look at him."

The man smiled. The light was hitting his thick glasses in such a way that Lucy couldn't see his eyes. Dust motes sizzled in a beam of sunlight from the window. Some music was playing, loud and anxious-sounding. Lucy didn't recognize it.

"My uncle's a photographer. He has some photos he took of him a week before he killed himself."

Lucy felt her sinuses prickling with tears the way they did when she told Rosie scary stories. Her mouth felt dry.

"You can come see if you want," he said. He handed Lucy a card.

She put it in her pocket and crumpled it up there, so he couldn't see.

❧

One of Emerson Solo's CDs was called *Imago*. The title song was about a phantom limb.

She wondered if when you died it was like that. If you still believed your body was there and couldn't quite accept that it was gone. Or if someone you loved died, someone you were really close to, would they be like a phantom limb, still attached to you? Sometimes Rosie was like another of Lucy's limbs.

❧

Rosie was the one who went—not Lucy. Lucy was aware enough of her own desire to escape so she did not let herself succumb to it. But Rosie still believed she was just looking for ways to be happier.

Blood Roses

❧

When Lucy got home from school and saw her sister's note she started to run. She ran out the door of thick, gray glass, down the cul-de-sac, across the big, busy street, against the light, dodging cars. She ran into the canyon. There was the place where the rattlesnake had blocked the girls' path, the turn in the road where they had seen the baby coyote, the grotto by the creek where the old tire swing used to be, where the high school kids went to smoke pot and drink beer. There was the rock garden that had been made by aliens from outer space and the big tree where Lucy had seen a man and a woman having sex in the branches early one Sunday morning. Lucy skidded down a slope causing an avalanche of pebbles. She took the fire road back down to the steep, quiet street. She got to the house just as Rosie knocked on the tall, narrow door.

Rosie was wearing a pink knit cap, a white frilly party dress that was too small, jeans, ruby slippers, purple ankle socks and a blue rhinestone pin in the shape of a large butterfly. No wonder people teased her at school, Lucy thought. She wanted to put her arms around Rosie, grab her hand and run but it was too late to leave because the man from the music store opened the door right away as if he had been waiting for them all that time.

He didn't ask them in but stood staring at them and twisting his mouth like he wanted to say something. But then another older man was standing at the top of the steep staircase. The girls couldn't see his face. He was whited-out with light.

Lucy knew two things. She knew that she and Rosie were going to go inside the house. She knew, too (when she saw it in a small alcove as she walked up the stairs), that she would take the screwdriver and put it in the pocket of her gray sweatshirt.

The walls were covered with plastic. So was all the furniture. Plastic was stretched taut across the floor. The walls were high, blond wood. There were skylights between the beams. Fuzzy afternoon sun shone down onto the plastic skins.

There was a long table. The older man stood at one end, watching. It was still hard to see what he looked like. The young man offered the girls pomegranate juice in small opalescent glasses. Lucy put her hand on Rosie's arm but her sister drank hers anyway.

Then Rosie walked out of the room.

"Rosie," Lucy whispered.

The young man said, "Do you know there's this dream that Jeffrey Dahmer had? He dreamed he was in this big, fancy hotel lobby with all these beautiful people wearing evening dresses and tuxedos. They were all pounding on the marble floor and screaming. But he was just standing there, not moving, not saying anything. He had on a leather jacket. He said it was like his skin."

Lucy felt for the screwdriver in her pocket. "I'm going to get my sister," she said.

But Rosie was back now. Her eyes looked brighter. She sat on a stool next to Lucy. She kept wetting her upper lip with her tongue.

The older man left the room.

"He's going to check on his photos," the

younger man said. "You didn't take anything, did you?"

Rosie shook her head, no.

"I have another story. It's about Richard Ramirez. When he went to this one lady's house, she kept him there like half an hour talking. Then he left. He didn't touch her. Do you know what she said to him? She said, 'My God, what happened to you?' And she listened. That was the main thing, she listened."

"What happened to you?" Lucy whispered.

The light in the room changed. It turned harsh. Emerson Solo was reclining on a chair. His skin was broken out, his hair was greasy, in his eyes, and he had a bottle in one hand. His long legs were stretched out in front of him. A blue butterfly was inside the bottle.

"Get the fuck out of here," the man from

Francesca Lia Block

the music store said, very softly. He was not looking at Lucy. The light was in his glasses. He was being swallowed up by the strange light.

Lucy felt the spell crack apart like an eggshell. She grabbed Rosie's hand. She pulled Rosie up from the stool. Rosie felt heavier, slower. Lucy dragged her sister out of the room. There was another staircase leading down to a back door.

Lucy flung herself down the staircase, pulling Rosie behind her.

"Lucy!" Rosie said.

A photograph had fallen out of Rosie's pocket. It was of Emerson Solo sitting on a chair with his legs stretched out in front of him.

Rosie tried to grab the photo but Lucy kept dragging her down the stairs. Their footsteps pounded, echoing through the house. Lucy fell against the door with her shoulder and jiggled the lock. The door opened.

They were in a strange, overgrown garden. Tearing through brambles. Lucy saw a crumbling stone staircase. She pulled Rosie down it, deeper into the bottom of the garden. A palm tree was wearing a dress of ivy. There was a broken swing moving back and forth. A white wrought iron bench looked as if it had been thrown against a barbed wire fence. The bougainvillea had grown over it, holding it suspended.

The barbed wire was very intricate, silvery. It was like metal thorns or jewelry. There was one small opening in the bottom. Lucy crawled through. Rosie followed her. But she stopped. Her ankle was wreathed in a circlet of silver spikes. Lucy dropped to the ground and carefully slipped the anklet off of her sister, not cutting her, not even catching her purple ankle socks.

She pulled Rosie to her feet. They were standing on the road, across from the wilds of the canyon. There were no cars. Not even the sound of cars. The sky was blue and cloudless. Lucy felt a buzzing sensation in her head like bees or neon.

She dragged Rosie across the road into the trees. The light kept buzzing around them.

Lucy reached into the pocket of her gray sweatshirt. It was empty. She reached into the other pocket and felt around. Nothing. The screwdriver was gone.

Gone, Lucy thought.

Rosie dropped to her knees on the soil.

"Lucy, look."

"What?" Lucy said. Her mouth felt numb, it was hard to talk.

"Blood roses."

"They don't grow here."

"I know that."

❧

The two sisters faced each other, waiting for the shivers to graze their arms, making the hairs stand up, but instead they felt only a strange, unnatural warmth as if spring had seeped into them and would stay there forever.

Giant

$\mathcal{S}$omething was wrong with Rachel Sorrow. Her limbs felt like sandbags, heavy enough to crush a small child. Her skin felt grainy. Her eyeballs strained with the intensity of a bulimic's and her mouth was dry. She lay with her head smashed against her bedroom door. Her feet against the opposite wall. Her neck ached, her fingers and toes tingled numbly. My, she had grown!

John Mandolin had chosen her to do his social studies project with him. It was about teenage suicide. They researched the topic together. She had gone over to his house after school. The magnolia trees were blooming big, waxy, white flowers. The eucalyptus trees were dripping their medicinal-smelling leaves onto the lawn. The light in his house was soft and melancholy. John Mandolin's parents weren't there, but his beautiful sister and her boyfriend were making out in her bedroom. Even the beauty of John Mandolin's sister intimidated Rachel Sorrow.

John Mandolin was sketching Rachel Sorrow as she sat on his bed under a David Bowie poster from the '70s. He was going to paint a portrait of her. She sat there wishing and wishing that she could be more beautiful.

Giant

Like her friend Berry Rodriguez. John Mandolin had a crush on Berry Rodriguez before he noticed Rachel Sorrow. Berry Rodriguez had a thick, long, brown ponytail and long brown legs. She almost never spoke. She scowled a lot. She was a brilliant ice-skater and rode horses on the weekends. Berry Rodriguez seemed more interested in horses than in boys, so John Mandolin had eventually given up on her. But Rachel Sorrow could not stop comparing herself to Berry Rodriguez whenever John Mandolin looked at her.

John Mandolin rode his bicycle every-where. He had very developed leg muscles, not unlike Berry Rodriguez's. He had straight blond hair that fell into his eyes. Blue eyes. Like Rachel Sorrow, he never let them take his picture for the school yearbook but she was sure it was for a different reason. Some noble, anticonformist reason rather than because he thought he would look stupid.

John Mandolin was the most beautiful boy that Rachel Sorrow had ever seen, not to mention the most beautiful boy who had ever shown interest in her, let alone the most beautiful boy, by far (the only one, actually), who had ever kissed her.

But the kiss had made her feel so strange. As she drove home through the streets of the darkening valley she could barely see for the tears. They slid down the sides of her face, cold on her hot cheeks. They trickled into her mouth, tasting of salt. Maybe her own tears were the poison that made her grow.

The metallic Santa Anas were rustling the

palm fronds and eucalyptus. Maybe the electricity in the air had contributed to the spell.

Rachel Sorrow's friend Sasha Sorenson won biggest flirt in middle school. She had soft blond hair and pretty green eyes, little teeth that showed coyly when she smiled and big dimples. When they graduated from middle school, three boys pledged themselves to her in the class will and testament. She lived in a house with lots of glass walls and a pool. Her mother was a fashion designer and her step-father was a photographer. She was always dressed in the cutest trendy clothes.

Rachel Sorrow's friend Elodie Sweet was tall and thin with dark skin and full lips and cascading gold-streaked brown curls. People said she could have been a model. She was a straight-A student and the best artist in her class. Like Sasha, she lived in a house with lots of glass walls and had a wardrobe so extensive that she and Sasha could wear matching styles every day of the week.

Sasha, Elodie and Berry went ice-skating at the mall after school. Then they sampled perfume at the department store counter and ate frozen yogurt at the ice cream place. On weekends they went horseback riding at the stables in the hills. Rachel Sorrow never joined them because she could not ice-skate or horseback ride.

Rachel Sorrow saw them at school and ate lunch with them in the quad. But it always felt as if they knew something she would never know, that they lived, somehow, in a private world of prismatic color, cherry lip gloss, shiny ice, frosty air and sleek-haunched creatures who knew more about sensuality than any boy. While Rachel Sorrow was turning into a giant.

Yes, that is what happened. After she returned home from John Mandolin's kiss she went into her bedroom, locked the door and began to grow.

The thickness of her limbs; oh, even her tongue felt thick! Her brain ached in her skull. Her heart had grown to be the size of a watermelon. It thudded heavily in her chest. (Unfortunately, the proportions of her body had not changed; she was still flat on top and a little pear-shaped through the hips.)

What are giantesses? Rachel Sorrow had once read a story about a race of magical beings, earth spirits, who were driven underground by mankind, where they festered and fell into corruption. Some shrank and shriveled almost to nothing and others grew grossly huge; unable to move freely they had to lie in the muck and mud, begging for someone to bring them roots and bones to gnaw on. Eventually they starved to death and the little people used their bones for shelter. Rachel Sorrow didn't know if she was one of these sorts of giantesses and what the deal was with John Mandolin. She wondered if he ever kissed her again, would that break the spell or make it worse? And, of course, he would never kiss her again, now. Even if Berry Rodriguez was not an obstacle (at least in Rachel Sorrow's mind). He would never paint her, he would never do a social studies project with her and he would never kiss her. She was revolting. She was much, much too much.

Giant

That was what her English teacher wrote on all her creative assignments, "Too much." Or at least, "A bit too much." Rachel Sorrow knew she was too much. She had way too many feelings. For instance, she was already in love with John Mandolin, just based on the fact that he had painterly talents, bicyclist's legs, the lips and heavy-lidded eyes of a Byzantine angel, and compassion for teenagers who contemplated suicide. If she and John Mandolin started dating, Rachel Sorrow would be compelled to write him love poetry every night. She would want to make out with him every night. She would climb in his window. She would weep into his shirt. He would say, "You are so intense. Like a storm. It's shocking how intense you are." She would get bigger and bigger every time they kissed until she crushed him with her lips and mashed him to bits with her teeth.

What, you may ask, became of this girl named Rachel Sorrow? Did she ever go back to her normal size? Did she shrink to the size of an elf and find a way to crawl into John Mandolin's pocket for the rest of her living days? Did she go storming through the halls of her high school, trampling the mean kids who called her names? Did John Mandolin graduate, go on a bicycle tour of the United States, settle down in Oregon and start a business hand painting racing bikes? Did he marry a giantess who lay with him in the countryside, her body his bed? Did he say, "You are too much, way, way, too much, go away, too intense, you feel more intensely about me than I will ever feel about you"? Or did he find a beautiful, sensitive woman his own size, someone who had learned to manage her emotions appropriately? What happened to Berry, Sasha and Elodie? Are they still friends? Were they one another's bridesmaids? In pastel dresses or black dresses? Did they go into medicine? Sports? The arts? Are they still married or divorced? How pretty are their daughters? How self-contained? When Rachel Sorrow grew huge, did her mother bring her supper on a tray like Max's mother in *Where the Wild Things Are*? Did Rachel Sorrow cry so many tears thinking of all these things, as well as of her great-grandmother's death in the Holocaust, that she drowned herself when she shrank to normal size, not unlike Alice in Wonderland? Did she shrink to normal size? Graduate? Fall in love? Get married? Have children? Divorce? Fall in love again?

What shall we do, all of us? All of us passionate girls who fear crushing the boys we love with our mouths like caverns of teeth, our mushrooming brains, our watermelon hearts?

My Haunted House

$\mathcal{F}$leurette believed that her doll-house was haunted. There had been a number of disturbing incidents. The tiny china plates from the glassed-in corner cabinet had all fallen on the floor and smashed. Which could have been attributed to an accident or a minor earthquake tremor but she was sure this was not the case.

The real electric lights would flicker on and

off at night. This could have been attributed to an electrical short but she was sure this was not the case.

When the dollhouse baby was found flung out on the floor, plastic limbs askew, Fleurette was sure that she was not mistaken.

Death lives in my dollhouse, thought Fleurette.

When she opened the front of the house, a cold draft blasted out at her. She ran to her mother, crying, but she could not articulate the problem. She was so sure her mother would not believe her. As a test, she told her mother stories all the time.

"There was a cow on the Petersons' lawn," she said.

"That's ridiculous," said her mother. "There are no cows in this neighborhood."

"I saw a blackbird with one blue eye."

"Fleurette, where did you get such an imagination?"

"My teacher eats chicken feet soup."

"Flurry, please stop telling tales," her mother said.

Can you imagine Mother's response to "My dollhouse is haunted; Death lives in my dollhouse"?

Fleurette knew it was useless to try.

Death could take many forms but in this case Death was a woman, very small, invisible, who lived in Fleurette's dollhouse. Death broke all the china plates because she did not need to eat and because it reminded her of earthquakes. She made the lights flicker because it reminded her of lightning. She considered lighting the birthday candles in the candelabra but if the house burned down she would have no place to live. Besides, she preferred cold temperatures. She did not believe in babies.

Fleurette had once loved that dollhouse. Her father had made it for her. He had even made most of the furniture. Fleurette and her mother had made the curtains and the pillows; they had wallpapered and carpeted. They had no idea that the tiny roses and fleur-de-lis and lace doilies and all the rest were decorations for Death.

Last Christmas the dollhouse family had a real Christmas tree and real birthday candles in the candelabra. Fleurette and her mother had wrapped tiny wooden blocks with shiny paper and thread to make presents. They made tiny stockings to hang on the mantelpiece and tiny real dough cookies to put on a plate for Santa Claus.

Fleurette's father was gone now. The dollhouse family still sat in the stasis of their Christmas dinner. Except for the baby who had been flung out of the house. Fleurette did not have the heart to put him back. Instead, she put him to sleep in a matchbox in her bedside table drawer. He looked dead.

Fleurette's teacher had sent her to the school nurse because she was bleeding. The school nurse sent her to the school counselor who called Fleurette's parents into her office. Then Fleurette had to meet with another lady who made her play with little dolls that reminded her of her dollhouse family. There was a mother, a father, a girl and a baby doll. A little while after that, Fleurette's father went away. Her mother said he was sick and he had to get better and then he would be back. Fleurette did not understand.

Fleurette went into the refrigerator and took out the pecan pie her mother had made. She scooped out the filling and ate it. It was creamy and tasted of burnt sugar. Then she ate a jar of pickles. Salty, crunchy. Then she ate some vanilla yogurt and a bag of rice cakes. Her tongue stung and her stomach felt full. But the food soothed her. It made her feel safe.

Meanwhile, Death was busy in the dollhouse. Death had turned all the mirrors around on the walls. Death had torn all the pages out of the books. Death had ripped up the tiny reproductions of the Matisse and the Cézanne and the Monet. Death had let in some mice; they chewed on the furniture and pooped their little black mice turds on the carpets.

Fleurette begged her mother to throw the dollhouse away but her mother refused. So the dollhouse was moved to the garage where Death continued to live because Death must live somewhere, mustn't she?

My Boyfriend Is an Alien

$\mathcal{M}$y boyfriend is an alien and this is a story about how I know.

I met my boyfriend while we were both photographing fires. The fires were sweeping the Santa Monica mountains and we had both parked on the Pacific Coast Highway at sunset to get some shots of the sky streaked with blood. My boyfriend was crouched in the brush with his camera. He had on a baseball cap over his shaved skull and little black-framed glasses. His shoulders were hunched protectively over the ribs that poked out under his T-shirt. Except for his eyes, he looked normal. But his eyes are much too big to be human. They are very long and wide. This is one way I know.

At the time my hair was pink and even though he pretended not to notice, it is my opinion that this attracted him to me, as aliens are interested in our colors, the way butterflies like certain flowers.

My boyfriend and I mumbled things about the fires but we didn't look directly at each other; we were looking at the sky. Then we skidded down the slope of rock and brush to get a different view. My photos looked like snapshots of a wildfire over a beach. His looked crazy beautiful, like the end of the world.

My Boyfriend Is an Alien

Afterward we went to eat burritos. My boyfriend had a carne asada burrito with extra hot sauce. I had a vegetarian bean and cheese with guacamole. My boyfriend is a carnivore. Aliens are not vegetarians. They like to eat cows cooked in various ways and other meats as well. He gnawed hungrily at his food and his big eyes flashed. I had mentioned that the fire photographs looked apocalyptic. He was telling me about the end of the world.

"The Mayan calendar ends on December 21, 2012," he said. "And it is so obvious that things are going in that direction. Look at your government! Look at the way they are treating nature and humanity! It is just so, so perverse."

I noticed that he didn't say our government. He had a slight accent but I couldn't figure out what it was. When I asked where he was from, he said, "All over. Far away." (!) His speech reminded me of poetry and sex.

"So what do you think will happen?" I asked, staring at his eyes. They were at least twice the size of mine.

"The world isn't necessarily going to explode. There will just be vast change. There is hope. It is in the rain forests, the healing plants from there, and in sex and the children who are being born. They have different strains of DNA. They aren't really human. So they will make the difference."

I didn't know what to say. Except I felt like fucking him when he said that. I took a bite of my burrito.

We went out other times. He always seemed to have cash. He took me to a little hole-in-the-wall Japanese place in West L.A. and ordered fried gizzard while I ate spinach with sesame seeds, a broiled rice ball, kabocha pumpkin, miso soup and lotus root.

"Do you know lotus root is supposed to be the food of the immortals?" I asked him. He tasted it respectfully but then went gleefully back to his gizzards.

This is one thing aliens like: animal flesh. They figure, why not? When in France . . . and all that. Besides, what is an organ that uses rocks to digest food when you are from outer space?

The first time we had sex was really something. My hair was bleached white. We were in the backseat of his 1965 VW bug at the beach. The stereo was playing Dead Can Dance. He likes that CD a lot. We were crunched into the backseat and he managed to get my clothes off without a struggle. I think he may have used his superpowers because one moment I was dressed and the next I wasn't. His own clothes came off the same way—baggy off-white cords and a black T-shirt that said "2012" on it, with an infinity symbol. He crushed into me with his body; it felt huge and heavy but also very light. I loved him so much at that moment. I wanted him to impregnate me with little alien babies but he was very conscientious with the condom. He put it on as gracefully and magically as the way he had undressed us. When he put himself inside me I started shaking and I couldn't stop. He was sweating all over me and he smelled like fire.

I didn't tell him that I had been hospitalized and that I had escaped. That I live with my crazy cousin and her boyfriend and a couple of

Hare Krishnas in a house in Venice. I didn't tell him that I've been diagnosed with schizophrenia or that I tried to kill myself with pills. That part of the reason I change my hair so often is so that I can forget who I really am. It didn't seem right to tell him these things. I didn't want to spoil the moment. We had such a good time when we were together.

Besides, when he touches me everything is okay. I don't want to hurt myself at all. I just want to kiss my alien boyfriend forever and ever. I need my body intact so I can do that.

I don't ask him about himself, either. He seems to prefer that. I don't know where he lives or where he gets his money. Once, when I hinted that I wanted to know more about his life, he said, "The only time is now. And now I'm here with you."

This time thing kind of drives me crazy. He never likes to make dates in advance. He says he doesn't understand our calendar; it doesn't make sense. He doesn't call me or email me but if I call him and ask him to come play with me, he always says yes.

Finally, one time, I said to him, "If there is a draft, will you take me to your planet?"

He said, "Sure, baby, whatever you want."

"Can I have your baby?" I asked him. "It would be so cute. It would have such big eyes!"

"We'll have to see about that," my boyfriend said.

"Maybe the condom will break," I said.

I've changed my hair again. It is black with bleached skunk stripes. Tomorrow we are leaving; I just know it. We are going to get away from this place before the whole experiment explodes. We are going to get into his spaceship and fly to his planet. He lives in the hollow core where no one can find us. Time is different there. The moment is so perfect in itself that you don't need to think ahead or behind. We will have little alien babies with big eyes, big heads, big brains, big hearts that are filled with compassion. On his planet there are no words for schizophrenia, suicide or war.

That's where I'm going.

Horses Are a Girl's Best Friend

*B*erry liked animals more than humans. Who wouldn't? Animals don't see what you look like. They don't care. They respond to your essence. They value you for who, not what, you are. Berry was used to boys falling in love with her because of the shiny brown ponytail on the top of her head. Because of the sunny brown clear color of her skin. Because of the size of her breasts and the length of her legs. But none of the boys seemed to care about who she was inside. And even if they cared, they would have to go through so much to find out. They would have to ask her so many questions. Animals never ask questions; they just know.

Berry went horseback riding every weekend. She drove her VW bug on the freeway, into the hills of Hollywood. Into the trees. There were stables at Griffith Park and Berry rode her horse down the dusty trails. She wore Levi's and cowboy boots. She liked the feel of the animal, sleek and muscular between her thighs. She loved the warm-straw smell of the horse and the way he responded to her voice and her movements. Sometimes it really did seem as if they were one creature.

Her friends stopped coming with her. They were more interested in boys and shopping now. She liked to be away from their gossip and their chatter. And from her house, from her three brothers who were always taking the remote away and screaming at her to get out of the bathroom. They treated her like some kind of mutant who had invaded their world of baseball and automobiles with her distracting hair and torso. They put posters of skinny blondes in bikinis up on the doors of their rooms as one might put up crosses and bulbs of garlic to scare away vampires.

One day Berry was cantering along all alone. The sky was gray; the air smelled of smoke. Her ponytail bounced on her back. The city, with its people who saw you but didn't know you, who touched you but didn't feel you, who heard you but didn't understand you, was far away.

And then, there he was.

There he was and she would always remember him standing at the curve of the road with his black hair and his flared nostrils and his gap-toothed smile and his goatee and his sunglasses and his white undershirt. Just like any other boy. Except he wasn't.

Because he wasn't riding his horse.

They were silent for a while.

"You a Valley girl or what?"

"What?"

"You look a little like a Valley girl." He gestured to the top of her head where the ponytail was fastened with a scrunchy. "The . . . the thing."

"And who are you, homey?"

"East L.A., man."

"Uh-oh."

"What's that supposed to mean?"

"Big tough guy."

"Yeah, I'm tough. But I can be sweet. That's what the ladies tell me."

At this point he was not making a good impression. He was more man than animal and it didn't sit well.

It did cross her mind, though, if she were honest—it did cross her mind that it would be awkward but extremely interesting to have sex with him. She had not had sex with a boy before. Everyone thought she was a scared, uptight virgin but it really had to do with the issue that boys did not perceive essence and so, then, what was the point in making love, which was all about essence, or at least should be?

They rode for a while (rode, she thought, is that the right term?). He was whistling between his teeth—some song she had heard on KROQ or something. He even played a little air guitar without realizing he was doing it. She was jealous that he didn't need the use of his hands. His biceps were developed and the veins protruded a little along the ridge of muscle.

"So what do you do in the Valley, girl?"

"What do you do in the barrio, homes?"

"Hey!"

"Well!"

"Okay, what do you do?"

She shrugged, embarrassed all of a sudden. Like she should be embarrassed!

"Come on, tell me. I won't laugh at you."

"I ice-skate."

"Ooh, skater girl. You got the legs. What else? Do you go to the mall with your friends?"

"So?"

"I'm just asking. What do you want be when you grow up? An ice-skater? A cowgirl?"

"A vet," she said, not unaware of the way it might affect him.

"And I don't think you mean as in Vietnam. Desert Storm. Persian Gulf. Iraq."

"No, I mean like taking care of animals." She couldn't help emphasizing the last word. She thought he winced a little.

"Why that?" He was serious now and his voice was softer.

"I like them better than people. People don't shut up."

They rode silently for a while. He swatted a fly on his arm. His nostrils flared. His back haunches rippled.

"I have to go," she said.

"Okay, Doc. See you again sometime."

❧

They met every Saturday after that, in the same place on the trail. Miraculously, no one else was ever there. They rode in silence most times listening to their breath.

This was enough for her. In fact, this was better than anything. This was better than when he spoke and tried to be a man.

❧

He told her a few things, though. He told her that he had to stay in his mother's basement most of the time. That his family felt shame. But at the same time his hombres revered him in some way. They considered him their mascot, if a bit of a freak. They held their meetings in his red-lit basement. Drinking beer, playing cards, rapping and showing off tattoos. At one point they had all gotten matching tattoos of a man-horse somewhere on their backs.

❧

One night she woke up and a man was standing in her room. Before she could scream out, someone had a hand over her mouth.

She thought, Not. Like. This.

The man said, "I won't hurt you. I'm with your friend. He got hurt real bad."

When she stopped struggling the man led her gently to the window. A truck was parked on the quiet street. The man shone a flashlight at the truck and someone inside put on another light for a second, long enough for Berry to see someone she recognized in the back of the truck.

❧

He was bleeding from his flank. His eyes were glassy and his breathing shallow. She knelt beside him and ran her fingers across the bridge of his nose. It was broad with a little bump.

"No," she whispered.

"I'm going to be okay," he said. "You're going to fix me up and then we are going to be married and have all these little babies galloping around the house."

But he was weak by now. A pale sheen of sweat glazed his forehead. She said to his friends, "We have to call someone."

"No way. We can't call someone. Look at him. What are we supposed to say?"

She cleaned him up as best she could and they told her to sew up the wound but she was too scared. She'd never done anything like that. They said to use a needle and thread and they'd pour alcohol on it. He was delirious by this time. She was crying.

By morning he was gone. They drove away and she still had his blood on her hands. Later, she would tell herself it was a hallucination, all of it. How could it be real? There are no centaurs in Los Angeles. And gang members from the east side do not venture into the Valley to swear their love to even the loveliest of lonely girls.

Skin Art

*E*lodie Sweet did not think she would ever get a tattoo. Even when she fell in love with Darby who had a tattoo parlor on the east end of Melrose. She always imagined what people's tattoos would look like when they were seventy years old. The saggy inked flesh. It just didn't feel right to her.

Rachel said, "You might not even live that long."

Sasha said, "They have lasers that'll remove those things now. If you change your mind."

Elodie said, "The whole point is not to change your mind. It's supposed to be forever. That's the whole point."

Berry smirked primly; she would never get a tattoo!

Both Sasha and Elodie liked to wear startling clothes and they had even gotten their noses pierced. But tattoos were a different thing; you couldn't just let the skin grow back!

Darby had tattoos all over his arms and chest and back like a shirt. He had devils and angels and roses and lilies and serpents and tigers and dragons and scorpions and butterflies and bleeding hearts and skulls and mermaids.

Elodie had met Darby when she was shopping on Melrose with Sasha. They were wearing their matching lace petticoats over black tights and black combat boots. They saw Darby at a magazine stand and were impressed by his Mohawk. He asked to take their picture for his MySpace page. Then he gave them his card and showed them his tattoos. He and Elodie started emailing each other after that. It turned out they liked the same early punk bands, films (*The Decline of Western Civilization* and *Blade Runner*) and artists (she loved that he had Frida Kahlo as one of his top MySpace friends).

Darby was from the Midwest but he'd gone to art school in New York. Then he came to L.A. and opened his tattoo parlor. Now he was twenty-four. He told Elodie Sweet that she was beautiful and had the perfect name but was too young and that she should find a nice underage guy to hang out with.

Elodie told Darby that age was only an abstraction, like time, and that what mattered was how two souls connected. Darby told Elodie that even having sex with her wasn't worth going to jail.

Elodie responded to this in a way that no one, not even her closest friends, ever would have expected. She stopped dressing up in outfits that matched Sasha's. She stopped listening to music and going shopping. She stopped ice-skating and horseback riding. She ate raw cookie dough and then went on long runs by herself in the hills to burn off the calories. She drew pictures of herself and Darby on adventures all over the city. It was an ongoing comic strip on its way to becoming a graphic novel. Except it had no plot. It was just Elodie and Darby being in love in different locations. On the carousel at the Santa Monica Pier. On the carousel in Griffith Park. In the fountain at the Hollywood Bowl. On the boardwalk at Venice Beach. At the Magic Castle and Yamashiro's restaurant in the low hills of Hollywood. At the Theatricum Botanicum in Topanga Canyon.

And then, a plot came to her.

Elodie woke up one morning with a tattoo. It was a tattoo of a red rose on her hipbone and on the densely clustering petals it said "Darby." Her first thought was that he had snuck in, in the middle of the night, drugged her and done it while she was sleeping. It looked just like his work. But how could she have slept through all that? And she didn't feel hung over or in pain. The tattoo had just materialized on her skin.

She showed it to Sasha who thought it was

cool and, because Sasha believed in those things due to her own rather improbable life, insisted that it was a manifestation.

"It happened by itself because you are so in love with him. Your body did it."

"I like the idea of him sneaking in my window and drugging me a lot better."

"Well, at least it's pretty and in a discreet place," Sasha said. "When you get a boyfriend you can cover up the name with another leaf."

I'm not going to get another boyfriend, Elodie thought, but she didn't say it. She believed tattoos were for keeps.

Days passed and she kept her rose hidden. It comforted her. At night she stood naked in front of the mirror looking at it. It emphasized her long torso and the slender curve of her hips. The privacy of her pelvis. It looked just like something Darby would have done. She wanted to email him and tell him but she knew it would sound too crazy.

Then one morning Elodie stepped out of the shower and caught a glimpse of color in the mirror.

It was a giant lotus blossom on her lower back.

She called Sasha. "This is getting creepy," Sasha said.

"Getting?"

"Yeah. This is really f-ing creepy."

"What am I supposed to do?"

"Is it pretty?" Sasha asked.

"It's gorgeous."

"I guess you don't do anything," Sasha said. "At least it's not a bong."

There was a D.A.R.E. urban legend that

was going around their school about a boy who got high and had his friend tattoo a picture of a bong on his chest. It was huge, lopsided, blurry and gruesomely ugly.

This did not make Elodie feel better.

She worked on her comic strip. In it, she started manifesting tattoos. At least it was a plot.

And in real life the tattoos kept coming. A Tibetan goddess was sitting cross-legged on the lotus flower. Butterflies swarmed around her. Stars hung over her head. Wild animals slept at her feet.

Elodie was not that big. The tattoos soon covered all of her slender back, shoulders and hips. One morning her arms wore lace sleeves. Morning glories and oleander blossoms were clambering over her shoulders toward her breasts. A pretty but lascivious-looking fairy with battish wings flew across her abdomen. Elodie put on a long-sleeved black turtleneck and drove out of the Valley, through Laurel Canyon, down Melrose to Darby's tattoo parlor.

He looked up at her when she walked through the door. He had bright blue eyes that felt invasive. The sides of his head were freshly shaved.

"Did you finally decide to let me do you?"

"Very funny," she said.

"Sorry. Tattoo you."

She stepped closer to him. The air conditioner in the store was broken and a little fan whirred. They were both sweating. Especially Elodie in the turtleneck. In the back room she could hear the buzz of someone's needle.

Elodie took off her shirt and flung her arms in the air. Her breasts were small and upturned, framed by flower tendrils. She pivoted around and then dropped her arms to her sides.

"Holy shit. Who did those?"

"I did."

"Put on your shirt," he said.

He took off his own and went to cover her with it. She pulled away from him.

"You could get me shut down," he said. He looked at his naked chest and put his shirt back on.

She put her hands over her face. Her back with its Tara, its garden, was shaking. He helped her put her shirt on again. He stood watching her, but not touching, like she was the goddess on her back come to life—beautiful but terrifying.

Skin Art

"Talk to me," he said.

(Every girl loves to hear those words from the right man. It is possible those words are the greatest seduction line ever. Especially if they are said without any ulterior motive, as Darby said them then.)

Elodie told him that the tattoos had appeared. "You better help me," she said. "At first I thought it was cool. Then I thought I was just going crazy. Now I'm scared they are going to grow onto my face. Onto my cheeks and lips! I'm not a freak!"

"Of course, you're not," he said gently.

"I can't help it if I want to be with you. It's not my fault."

"You are going to like a lot of guys, Elodie Sweet."

"Shut up! You're the freak. Shut up!"

"Come on," he said.

She followed him to his apartment in the hills of Silverlake. It was in a rickety little bungalow overlooking the water. A string of colored Christmas lights hung across the porch and there was an outdoor fireplace surrounded by bougainvillea. Inside, the walls were a collage of images torn from magazines. There were Balinese shadow puppets, conch shells, Buddha statues, Hindu goddesses, African carvings, candlesticks encrusted with wax drippings. His bed was in a corner, dimly lit, under a crowded bookshelf. She wondered if he ever worried about earthquakes.

It is amazing to think of how little it takes to make a girl, of a certain age and artistic temperament, believe she is in love.

"Come here," he said.

Skin Art

It was not exactly what she had hoped for or even expected. He was sweet but rough and he didn't look into her eyes. Afterward, he put on the TV. It was the Independent Film Channel, but still.

Elodie went home. The tattoos began vanishing, one by one, fading to stretch-mark-like shadows on her tawny skin and then nothing at all.

A year later, by the time she was away at college, even his name was gone.

My Mother the Vampire

*A*t that time, Sasha did not know that she could sing. Sasha's house was like a Jetsons cartoon. The furniture was '60s space-age plastic. The lighting was low and frosty. Some of the light fixtures were shaped like stars and constellations. There were round chairs that spun in circles and big glass walls overlooking a kidney-shaped pool. Dreamy, lyricless music was always playing from speakers hidden in the walls. There was a fully stocked bar and a big screen TV. Everyone liked to hang out there. Elodie and Berry came over and the girls lay in the sun and painted their toenails. Sasha always used the most extreme shades of nail polish. She liked greenish black and neon orange. Elodie liked deep reds and Berry liked neutrals. They drank diet sodas and ate salads with iceberg lettuce, cherry tomatoes and Thousand Island dressing. Sometimes they invited boys over. The boys all had a crush on Sasha because Elodie and Berry were not interested in them but Sasha always gave them her biggest dimpled grin and lifted her breezy hair to let them put suntan lotion on her back. They did goofy dives off the diving board and threatened to pull the string of her bikini top. They raided her kitchen for chips, salsa and beer. Elodie and Berry rolled their eyes but Sasha just gave them her smile again, peeking out at them from under strands of blond hair as she painted her tiny toenails vile colors that managed, on Sasha, to appear coy and cute.

One of the boys was named Clyde Carrera. He had thin brown hair that was always falling into his olive green eyes, a long face and a dimple in his chin. He had a little crackly voice that sounded like it was changing from a boy's voice to a man's, but never quite did. Sasha sometimes let him paint her toenails or give her back rubs and sometimes she even kissed him but then she sent him away saying she just wasn't ready. Clyde Carrera liked Sasha so much that he did what she asked, went home, masturbated with a pair of underpants that he had stolen from her drawer, and then came back to put suntan lotion on her skin and let her put his hair in pigtails if she wanted.

Sasha's mom, Bets, was rarely around so the kids could go wild at Sasha's house. Bets was a former model. She was rather shockingly beautiful. Black hair flowed to her waist. Her eyes were a violent blue. Everyone assumed she did a lot of Botox and Restylane. She looked more like Sasha's sister, especially when she was dressed in her Juicy sweats or her baby doll tops with jeans and ballet flats, her hair in a ponytail. In fact, people would often say, "Is that your sister?" It made Sasha uncomfortable.

Sasha's mother said things like, "Sasha is so pretty. She's really got the looks. Luckily, because she struggles with other things. Like school. But looks will get you far in this world."

She said these things in front of Sasha, and sometimes to strangers.

Once she said them in front of Clyde Carrera who got drunk and told Sasha her mother was a bitch and he wanted to rescue Sasha from her and bring her home to live with him and sleep in his baby sister's room.

Sasha told Clyde never to call her mother names. She told him not to bother coming back to swim in her mother's kidney-shaped pool and drink her mother's beer ever again.

❧

Sasha lost a lot of weight and her friends were worried that she might be bulimic because as far as they could see she was always eating. She ate pizza and steak and french fries and donut holes. She even switched from diet sodas to regular. But she was getting skinnier and skinnier and there were dark shadows under her eyes like eye shadow put on upside down. Sasha promised her friends that she wasn't vomiting behind closed doors in the mirror-paneled bathroom. She said she just had a high metabolism, like her mother, and told them not to worry.

Clyde Carrera came over late one summer night with flowers—daisies and orange lilies. The warm air made the scent of the flowers and the chlorine from the pool more intense. Through the glass walls the water glowed with its own blue haze. Bets was out as usual and Sasha was alone, wearing a boy's T-shirt and fuzzy slippers shaped like white cats and watching a Madonna concert.

Sasha wondered what it would be like to have Madonna as your mother. She loved

Madonna's wardrobe and how she transformed herself all the time and how she adopted a baby from Malawi. She knew that Madonna had a special machine at home that gave her oxygen facials so she would never look old.

Sasha let Clyde in because the Madonna concert was depressing her, because of the flowers and because she missed putting his hair in pigtails. She gave him a beer and he fed her Cherry Garcia ice cream from her mother's freezer, out of the carton with a turquoise plastic spoon. He said he thought she should stop losing weight, that she was just perfect. Then he gave her a foot massage that made her squeal with pleasure and almost made him come. Clyde kissed Sasha's feet, her ankles, her slim calves and thighs. She whispered, "I know you picked those flowers from my mother's garden," before she let him kiss her farther up.

It was like a transfusion.

❧

Every night after Sasha turned thirteen Bets came to her daughter's bedside. Bets hummed a little tune as she tied the tourniquet around Sasha's slender arm. Then Bets patted Sasha until a frail blue vein stood out and Bets stuck the needle in. It didn't hurt much. There was usually only a tiny speck of blood where the needle went in and rarely a bruise. Afterward, Bets gave Sasha a Hello Kitty, Barbie or Disney Princess Band-Aid and a lollipop. Sasha's tongue was orange or green or bright red and she had bright sugared bits stuck in her molars. The dentist began finding a lot of cavities so Sasha started getting up and brushing her teeth after the lollipop, although her mother never suggested this. By then, Bets was asleep, next to Sasha in Sasha's double bed.

She slept like a languid teenager, well-fed on her daughter's vivifying fluids.

Clyde wanted to take Sasha away with him when he graduated and moved to Seattle to go to art school. She said she couldn't leave her mother. Clyde emailed her for a while but when she stopped writing back he gave up and dated Marcy Parks who was physically Sasha's exact opposite and who he would later marry.

Sasha seemed like such a sweet girl with such a nice upbringing. Yes, her mother was a little narcissistic but so are other L.A. moms and not all their daughters start shooting heroin at nineteen. No one could understand either (though they were impressed) when, at twenty-seven, having cleaned up her act, Sasha became the head of the needle exchange program in downtown Los Angeles.

By then, Sasha had finally moved out of her mother's house. She got a cottage in Silverlake with roses in the courtyard and sunny windows. All of the furniture was from thrift stores and looked nothing like something out of a cartoon. Sasha spent a lot of time alone recording songs she had written and putting them up online. They were catchy tunes, reminiscent of the early eighties. People said Sasha's voice was a little like a happy Debbie Harry's. In spite of the upbeat sound the lyrics were frustratingly obscure and dark. But the more depressing the lyrics Sasha wrote, the happier she felt.

Sasha never really blamed Bets. She understood and, after all, someday she might be a mother, too. It is hard to be a pretty girl in this world. It is hard to be a woman growing old.